The Flashboat

Also by Jane Cooper

Green Notebook, Winter Road
(1994)

Scaffolding: Selected Poems
(1984, 1993)

Threads: Rosa Luxemburg from Prison
(1978) (chapbook)

Maps & Windows
(1974)

Calling Me from Sleep
(1974) (chapbook)

The Weather of Six Mornings
(1969)

for Tony

The Flashboat

Poems Collected

and Reclaimed

Jane Cooper

Jane Cooper

W·W·Norton & Company

New York   London

For information about permission to reproduce selections from this book, write to
Permissions, W. W. Norton & Company, Inc., 500 Fifth Avenue, New York, NY 10110

The text and the display of this book are composed in Granjon
Composition by Allentown Digital Services
Manufacturing by Haddon Craftsmen
Book design by Margaret Wagner

Library of Congress Cataloging-in-Publication Data

Cooper, Jane, 1924–
    The flashboat : poems collected and reclaimed / Jane Cooper.
        p.   cm.
    Includes index.
    ISBN 0-393-04777-6
    I. Title.
PS3553.O59A6   1999
811'.54—dc21   99-31822
                                                    CIP

W. W. Norton & Company, Inc., 500 Fifth Avenue, New York, N.Y. 10110
www.wwnorton.com

W. W. Norton & Company Ltd., 10 Coptic Street, London WC1A 1PU

1 2 3 4 5 6 7 8 9 0

For Grace, Adrienne, Jean

Contents

Maps & Windows (*1974*)

Scaffolding: *Poems 1975–1983 (1984)*

Foreword

Poetry seems to me one of the rare, perfectly free human activities available to us. Accordingly, I have not hesitated to change my work in small ways over the years. But basically, this book is a record of my life in poetry as that record has gone out into the world. If the original self-definitions have been subject to some redefinition, that is part of a lifelong effort to be more honest, to understand a fluid nature in the grip of a difficult century. And perhaps after all the pattern is not so unusual for a woman artist of my generation.

My first collection, *The Weather of Six Mornings,* was not published until 1969, when I was forty-four. Essentially, it consisted of poems from my thirties and a revelatory moment just beyond. *Maps & Windows,* published in 1974, brought together poems of my forties with a group of previously unpublished poems from my twenties under the title "Mercator's World." *Scaffolding* (1984) was the selection of my fifties. *Green Notebook, Winter Road* (1994) came out just in time for my seventieth birthday.

Since then I've had occasion to go through many old drafts of published poems and still more drafts of poems that were never published in book form. In the case of the published poems, I've found some lines, generally from the time of first composition, that I like better than those that were originally printed, and so I've made a few substitutions. In *Scaffolding,* I had already included a section of "reclaimed" poems—poems that could have been part of earlier books but were left out. In this volume, I've added eighteen more of the "reclaimed," but instead of boxing them together I've inserted them in the ongoing, rough chronology of the published work, as nearly as possible according to when they were written. I see now that when such poems were omitted, it was sometimes because they seemed too personal, at other times because they were rather loosely written. Now, it's my hope that read in context they will above all add to the humanness of the story all the poems tell.

Also, because both *The Weather of Six Mornings* and *Maps & Windows* opened with what was most recent, I've rearranged the order of sections within those books to make for an easier narrative or time line. Details of such changes along with a list of the previously unpublished poems can be found in the Notes.

The earliest poems here were written out of the aftermath of World War II, and while few of them mention the war directly, I was haunted by a sense of blitz, Holocaust, the vast camps for "displaced persons," the vague movement of whole populations. This sense could be likened to a giant searchlight, setting the domestic in harsh perspective. *The Weather of Six Mornings* was a largely personal, domestic book, but the skeptical feminism of the "Mercator's World" poems reappeared in poems of the late sixties and seventies, especially "Threads." I owe a great deal to the women's movement, which has enabled me to speak of what once seemed incommunicable. Poetry has been my community. The fellowship of women writers and other women artists in particular has assured me I could be heard.

    Green Notebook, Winter Road dealt specifically with the lives of girls and women, with aging, friendship, illness, the humor and "complex shame" of a white Southern heritage, the enduring mystery of art. Mystery and clarity: these have been my concerns from the beginning. The mystery of our existence on earth. The clarity of a moment's elucidation which is the poem. Always I have been more interested in the role of time in a writer's work than in any given theme. "Vocation: A Life" traced the changes and repetitions in one woman's dreaming through youth, childhood, middle and older age. Now, without my having chosen it exactly, *The Flashboat* turns out to have the same structure, from its first confident morning statement to "Poverty, solitude / have strangely flowered" and "light by which the writing / was composed."

A few years ago I wrote, "We are not separate. And the work for all of us must begin, I think, with the stripping down of words, with listening, with acknowledging our fear, with getting back to origins, with learning to live, however perilously, in this moment, for it is our only life." Poems are moments of the most acute consciousness. Through them we reckon with the *now* and *here,* and yet we enter into a dialogue with history and otherness. No one of my poems can possibly satisfy all the ideals I have for it. And yet to have been allowed these years, always in touch with the thought of what poetry can be, and the struggle to make more truthful poems, seems an incomparable gift.

Poems are made in solitude, but they move toward connectedness. Poetry calls me back to who I am; simultaneously, it releases me into a mode of being that is larger and more strenuous, in which the self is challenged only to be let up, a little changed.

The Weather
of Six Mornings

Poems

1954–1967

(1969)

Morning on the St. John's

The Chinese character for landscape is mountains-and-water.
A Japanese image of heaven is Fuji reflected in a pool.

This is a country where there are no mountains:
At dawn the water birds like lines of rain
Rise from the penciled grasses by the river
And slantwise creak across the growing light.
The sky lifts upward and the breath of flowers
Wakes with the shadows of the waking birds.

The shadows of the birds, the dancing birds!
With so much freedom who could ask for mountains?
The heron stands here ankle-deep in flowers,
Wet hyacinths that burn more blue with rain,
And waves of smaller wings hurl wide the light
All up and down the horizontal river.

And now the sun shakes blue locks in the river
And rises dripping-headed while the birds
Go wild in curves of praise at sudden light.
The fire that would flash instantly off mountains
Bathes this round world in dew as dark as rain
And then strikes green and gold among the flowers.

The dropping heads, the smooth and shaken flowers!
(Among the grasses, blue eyes by the river,
And in the garden, fires after rain.)
Under umbrella leaves the mockingbirds
Still nestle and trill quietly of mountains,
Then whistle Light!—cadenza—Light! and Light!

While higher and higher sweeps the opening light
In bluish petals as of opening flowers,
More pure than snow at dawn among the mountains.
Paler than any flush along the river,
Beyond the reach of eyefall flight of birds,
It floods a sky swept innocent by rain.

The assault of sun, the long assault of rain—
Look how our darkness is made true by light!
Look how our silence is confirmed by birds!
The mind that pastured ankle-deep in flowers
Last night, must wake to sunrise on the river,
Graze wide and then grow vertical as mountains;

For even a glimpse of mountains fogged with rain
Or mirrored in a river brings delight
And shakes us all as dawn shakes birds and flowers.

JACKSONVILLE, FLORIDA

Leaving Water Hyacinths

from an old photograph, Jacksonville, 1933

I see you, child, standing above the river
Like a thin bush, too young for bloom or fruit
But solidly planted, both knees locked backwards
And blue-gray eyes quietly, typically watchful:
The catboats play over a chuckling sunlight
(Funny how waves slide over, sunlight under!)
And hyacinths grip down, rooted in heaven.

I know—because you become me—you say goodbye
To thumping dark paddle-like hyacinth leaves
With blood-brown stems and blue and sucking heads,
To the river's massive purr, its sustained dredge
And flap at the dock stilts (stiff, a heron's legs)—
Sounds which can stop in air your breakfast teaspoon
Or lap as lights across the bedtime ceiling.

I know—because you contain me—you seem cool-eyed
And yet you sense that once you leave this landing
Your whole life after will be sailing back:
A seeking out of losses, the catboats' débris
Which cloud a harbor but bloom upwards blue,
And where the heron climbs, his lank limbs dropping,
Music that cradles grief to an Atlantic.

The Faithful

Once you said joking slyly, *If I'm killed*
I'll come to haunt your solemn bed,
I'll stand and glower at the head
And see if my place is empty still, or filled.

What was it woke me in the early darkness
Before the first bird's twittering?
—A shape dissolving and flittering
Unsteady as a flame in a drafty house.

It seemed a concentration of the dark burning
By the bedpost at my right hand
While to my left that no man's land
Of sheet stretched palely as a false morning. . . .

All day I have been sick and restless. This evening
Curtained, with all the lights on,
I start up—only to sit down.
Why should I grieve after ten years of grieving?

What if last night I was the one who lay dead
While the dead burned beside me
Trembling with passionate pity
At my blameless life and shaking its flamelike head?

Blind Girl

I take your hand. I want to touch your eyes.
They are water-soft. I know. I could push them in.
Once a doll's eyes fell in before my fingers—
Instead of dropping tick-tock open and shut
They were cold holes like a poor frozen faucet.
Where does the water come from? I hear breathing.
Listen at the tap—you hear a kind of sobbing.

But your eyes have a panting kind of hush
And then a shudder like a huddled bird's
Lifting his neck-feathers in my two cupped hands.
That's the light in them, asking to get let out.
(Your lashes beat and beat against my fingers.)
And when we walk together, heat on my shoulders
Is soft as down, and that's a light called outside.

So seeing is something struggling to get out
To something like it, larger but more still,
And when you see, that must feel just like swimming.
I take your hand. There. Please let me hold you.
If I hold tight enough to your live fingers
It *must* work free. Oh, I could kill your eyes
Only to know a little more what love is.

For My Mother in Her First Illness, from a Window Overlooking Notre Dame

Why can I never when I think about it
See your face tender under the tasseled light
Above a book held in your stubby fingers?
Or catch your tumbling gamecock angers?
Or—as a child once, feverish by night—
Wake to your sleepless, profiled granite?

But I must reconstruct you, feature by feature:
Your sailor's gaze, a visionary blue,
Not stay-at-home but wistful northern eyes;
And the nose Gothic, oversized,
Delicately groined to the eyesockets' shadow,
Proud as a precipice above laughter.

Arrogant as a cathedral or the sea
You carry your blue spaces high and quick
On a young step, tapping or chivalrous.
Pilgrim of the ridiculous
And of a beauty now almost archaic,
I miss your swift inward, your needle's eye.

Light stalk, my love is all of movement,
Those ribs of quicksand feeling in your face,
Those knowledgeable, energetic gargoyles.
Still haunted by my first devils,
Alone and sick, lying in a foreign house,
I try to read. Which one of us is absent?

Snow in the City

Snow is a process of thinking. Down the street
I see the flakes ballooning from the west.
In eddies of wind they blow across the rooftops
And crash with soft violence on my windows,
The way that year the luna moths by hundreds
Brushed at our window, crackled and fell down;
Inside the room we trimmed our steady lamp.

I wonder how the cabin lies in winter
There on its hill, with all the ragged woods
Tangled below it. I can hear the snow
Hissing low down among those emptied vines,
The skeletons of summer berry parties;
It drags the spruce tree branches down until
Fine brushmarks ripple over all the footprints.

How many years? It must be seven since
I climbed that hillside in my city dress
And got those special calluses on my feet.
The things that you remember: not a plan
(The house, the hill, the berry vines and spruce,
A girl in heels climbing a paveless road)
But rather something like a magic lantern
(That sudden hedgehog raider in the night!)
A stepping into time as in a passage.

Looking through snow, you can't see the end of the street.

Rock Climbing

Higher than gulls' nests, higher than children go,
Scrambling and dangling to survey the sea,
   We crest the last outcropping strewn
     East of this island.

Now pell-mell, now stopping to pinch a finger
In an open fissure down which no sun glints,
   Where water gnaws and subsides, we comb
     As the tide rises

Each rock that locks us in a partial vision
Of the expanding, curved and eye-reflecting blue
   Which liberates but still hangs over
     Our minds' breathing.

As yet the gleams are steep and unexpected:
We study lichens like a dying scale,
   Silver as fishes; here crisp moss
     Moist in a crevice;

Then even lichens powder, and the rocks
Give way to sunny tables, dry escarpments,
   Each with its different texture, pocked
     Or smoothly sloping

Down to the pitch where barnacles or stain
Dark as a rust line show the heaving power
   Of water's shoulders, raised at night,
     Then wrested over.

And now the last rock! piled hugely up
And shoved to end a sprinkle like a jetty
   Of little boulders in the green-brown
      Irregular surface

Where seaweed shaped like coral swimming, kelp,
Pebbles and broken shells of clam or crab
   All shine or flicker up as down-watching
      We kneel and wonder.

Now balancing, laughing, brisk as children who
Spread out their arms and toe along a pole
   We skip from top to top, lift knees,
      Come out at angles

Until we have scaled it! stand aloft at last
With all the ocean for our freedom and
   Our meditation, all the swing
      Of limbs for glitter.

Warmed by the sun, tingling, with tired calves
And eyes of exultation we address
   The father of our knowledge, shrouded
      Faintly beyond us

At the lost line where wind is turned to water
And all is turned to light, dissolved or rinsed
   To silver where our eyes fish (gulls
      Sailing and falling

Out, out . . .). And now the seabirds call
Far off, recalled by memories like hunger,
    Screech and return, flying the tides
        Of pure air inwards

To where their nests are, intimate and cold;
While standing on those cliffs we slowly rest
    And looking back to hillsides build
        Imaginary houses.

DEER ISLE, MAINE

The Builder of Houses

What was the blond child building
Down by the pond at near-dark
When the trees had lost their gilding
And the giant shadows stepped
To the water's edge, then stopped?
With intent fingers, doing a boy's work
In a boy's old sweater,
She hammered against her dear world's dirty weather.

Proud of her first house
Which boasted an orange-crate ceiling,
A pillow, a stuffed mouse,
And room for complete privacy
In the obvious crotch of a tree,
She skipped and swagged; rude cousins came stealing
With boys' laughter
And dismantled all but one branchy rafter.

She hunted almost till summer
Before her second find:
A post like a sunken swimmer
Deep in the marsh where ducks
Made nesting clucks and squawks.
With cautious tappings she fashioned a duck blind—
Or so her stepfather
Claimed when his autumn guns began to gather.

All winter in secret mourning
She toiled on her third house.
Three miles from the driveway turning
Up a forgotten path,

Risking her mother's wrath,
She tramped until her footprints filled with ice.
That bright glazing
Revealed one day her high and forbidden blazing.

In the very swaying top
Of a windswept sugar maple
She had built a bare prop—
Five boards to hold the crouch
Of a fugitive from search.
Here on this slippery and hard-won table,
Armed with her hammer,
She was tracked down by dogs' and parents' clamor.

There was only one more trial:
When frozen, brackish March
Gave way to floods in April
She rowed a sadly leaking
Scow, its oarlocks creaking,
Out to an island in the glittering reach,
And there, halfheartedly,
Began to floor the bend of a stunted tree.

Why was this last, diminished
And never-mentioned mansion
The one she never could finish?
No one—not father nor mother
Nor even the mellowing weather—
Routed her from her chosen foothold and passion;
This time house and view
Were hers, island and vision to wander through.

But less and less she balanced
Her boat on the sunrise water

Or from her window glanced
To where that outline glimmered;
Island and house were inner,
And perhaps existed only for love to scatter
Such long, carefully planned
And sovereign childhood with its unrelenting hand.

For a Very Old Man, on
the Death of His Wife

So near to death yourself
You cannot justly mourn
For one who was beautiful
Before these children were born.
You only remember her
Poised by the edge of the sea
As you stalked heron-legged,
Chairing the baby high
(Red-capped, hilarious)
Through the ecstatic surf,
And all the boardwalk flags
Clapped to her seaward laugh.

Or perhaps she would pretend
To lose you over the edge
Of that great curve of blue
Distinct as a cliffy ledge,
And cry and wave and cry
Until with a little breath
She spied the red-capped head
Of the pledge both flung at death;
Then she would swing her hat
With her graceful arm held high
As if she would top the flags
And the flags could sweep the sky.

Now it is she who is gone
And you wait on the sand.
The place itself has changed,
The boardwalks are torn down.
For places curve with time
Over the horizon's rim;
Only a seabird flies
Lower and seems to skim

All that has been or is. . . .
No one is left to share
Those windless flags you see
Or praise her uncovered hair.

Bermuda

Old man, come out in the sun,
The white blind of one o'clock!
Across the road a rusty cock
Stalks, his wars forgotten.

Here red and purple hang
From trees and tropic sky,
A cockscomb sunblaze, high—
Or the rains clang

On tin roof and gutterspout
And hot palms whistling.
Old man, stop rustling
Your shaking plumes, step out!

For Thomas Hardy

(after reading "Nobody Comes," dated on my birthday)

But you were wrong that desolate dusk
    When up the street the crawl
    Of age and night grew tall
As a shadow-self leaning away
    From the gray religious husk
Of a streetlamp keeping watch above dead day.
    Another took some risk.

You thought yourself alone
    In a world whose nearest ghost
    Was the alien pentecost
Of strumming telegraph, the throb
    Of a motor quickly gone—
While over the animal sea my outraged sob
    Took life from the same dawn.

Practicing for Death

Monarch and fritillary, swallowtail—
Great butterflies red-brown or glossy black,
Spotted or striped or plain,
Each glistening with down—
I chased you through my earliest fields and back
Along a tangled track
To where the woods grew secret, dark and tall.

There you would disappear with a last hover,
Scurry or zigzag purposeless to the eye,
Witless and teasing, yet
Always beyond my net,
Beyond my fluttering hand that could not fly.
Brave alter-mystery,
Always you found some shadow for your cover.

Or I would watch you trembling on a branch
Open and close with pure control your wings
As if a steady hand
Slowly could wind, unwind
The coil that steeled those frail yet tensile springs,
As if unhurried breathings
Had drifted you aloft out of my reach.

Lost beyond reach—yet still I tried to follow
Down your close paths and into the sun again,
For what except to yield
All pleasures of the field
Into a single, gold and gathered grain?
To force the flash of vision
Under my grasp to fill that pulsing hollow?

And what if I garnered death, the fix of art,
Instead of the moving spark I chose to race?
When winter found my hoard
Pinned to a naked board,
Was it my own long-legged, sidelong grace
I had betrayed, the space
Of instant correspondence in the heart?

2

For there were times, after long hours spent
In meadows smelling hot and dry of noon
Where every grass would stir
Shagged over with blue aster,
I would surprise you, dozing, fumbling drone.
Quickly my sliding prison
Would muffle you in clouds of blinding lint.

And I would pinch my net around that weed
You hung from, until beating up and out
In dense, bewildered strivings
You battered with your wings
And head against the deep net's lightstruck throat,
Or loosening your feet
Crawled up the folded shadows of its side.

Then carrying you as hopefully as an egg
Cradled in cotton, I would pause, advance
On cautious legs until
I found someone to kill
The body I had pinioned in its dance—
Small, ignorant, intense
And homely engine of the whirligig.

Still in odd dreams I ponder, was it strength
Never to bear the final act of prey?
What native cowardice
Clamped me as in a vise
Before the oozing glamor of decay?
Elusive adversary,
I brought no stillness to your labyrinth.

Even the fields that beckoned then seemed wild,
Shimmering with sun-traps and cloud-plays.
I watch as you alight
And the old conquering fright
Fills up my throat. When shall I learn to praise
Tracing you down dark ways
Once more, live butterflies? ablaze, scared child!

Acceptances

1. The Sundial

Take out of time that moment when you stood
On the far porch, a monolith of man,
And I raised one flag arm above my head:
Two statues crying out in shapes of stone.

And take that moment when your flame-blue eyes
Blazed on me till true sunlight seemed to fail
And all our landscape fell away like lies:
The burr of bees, grass, flowers, the slow sundial.

And take that moment after kneeling speech
—*Rare things must be respected,* your lips said—
When moveless I withheld myself from reach,
Unmoving, gave my need to fill your need.

Behind us in the garden the great sundial
Began to stretch its shadow toward afternoon.
Nothing was altered. Only we sat still,
Spent with sane joy beyond the bees' numb drone.

2. The Graveyard

Where five old graves lay circled on a hill
And pines kept all but shattered sunlight out
We came to learn about
How each had sinned, loved, suffered, lost until
He met the other and grew somehow still.

Under those soughing, rumor-speaking trees
Full of dead secrets, on the August ground,
We leaned against a mound
Not touching; there, as we could, gave keys
To open midnight vaults that no one sees.

All that had shaped us thirty years or more
We tried to offer—not as brave youngsters do
Who need an echo, who
See in their fathers' sins a canceled score—
But as two grieving inmates tapping at the door.

Gifts of the self which were but bids for power,
Gifts of the innocent self—stripped, bound and torn—
A rare child wrongly born
And our best strivings turned, with age, half-sour:
Such darkness we unlocked within an hour.

Those five old graves lay speechless while the sun
Gradually stroked them with its flickering arm.
The smell of pines grew warm.
We walked away to watch a fresh stream run
As free as if all guilts were closed and done.

3. THE RACETRACK

Under our stillness fled the same low hooves—
After, before, from the first morning when
We stood to watch the horses exercise.
Like a small sea the track dazzled our eyes:
Two riders shouting, flattening to run,
A spray of turf flung glistening toward the sun,
Stallions and fillies combing like distant waves.

Blind, pounding beasts came whirling through the mist,
Sweat on their flanks, their ankles wreathed in spume,
The day I told you of my loneliness;
Or I saw darkly out of such distress
As knocked my heart against its fragile room
Until our eyes touched and that light went home—
So we were one before we spoke or kissed.

Now that our bodies move and wake as one
That daybreak dream of horses has changed too
And we are free to say, as shadows scatter,
Sound carries on this track as on deep water.
The trees shake out their leaves. We feel the slow
Rotation of a world in which we grow;
Slowly we learn our long wave's luminous motion.

In the Last Few Moments Came
the Old German Cleaning Woman

Our last morning in that long room,
Our little world, I could not cry
But went about the Sunday chores
—Coffee and eggs and newspapers—
As if your plane would never fly,
As if we were stopped there for all time.

Wanting to fix by ritual
The marriage we could never share
I creaked to stove and back again.
Leaves in the stiffening New York sun
Clattered like plates; the sky was bare—
I tripped and let your full cup fall.

Coffee scalded your wrist and that
Was the first natural grief we knew.
Others followed after years:
Dry fodder swallowed, then the tears
When mop in hand the old world through
The door pressed, dutiful, idiot.

A Little Vesper

Another day gone, and still
I haven't answered those letters
that clog my desk and heart.
The sky is a blown-up page
scribbled by swallows; the sun
drops in a pearl of mist
under an orange roof—
What am I hankering for?

Idly I hum this poem
as I wait for the tiny shriek
of a swallow outside, the whistle
of a leaf on my dry porch.
Sometimes it rains here. Letters
are piled up now like old snow
in the cramp of the spring evening—
Everyone sends their love.

And what do I want, ever,
more than these simple names
crying solicitude
from a black scrawl, beyond seas?
Swallows, it's time to fly home,
crawl in under the tiles
and bed with what we are—
breathe goodnight to the first strangers.

ROME

49

Roman Dream

She-death, my green mother, you
climbed invisibly toward me
up the black stairwell. I heard
you scratch, scratch, moistening
your lips as I tucked my skirt
tighter, sitting on the top
step, American, waiting.

Waiting for you to pass I
felt no fear. Behind me red-
gold Rome, rooftop café, my
lover, his woman, flowers. . . . Cold
stroked my throat. I thought, *No
one will know, no one in Rome
will ever know to find me.*

These High White Walls

So now to write the journal of this house,
these high white walls, this empty winter:
New scenes to disinter!
New ghosts to rouse!

Never a more stubborn dwelling-place
was bodied out with beds and chairs,
fleshed with familiars.
—Old empty face,

did you learn nothing from your dream of age?
Did no one laugh, make love or sing
to stamp your echoing
close with his image?

Let's call high festival, let's settle here,
break bread, kiss gently and converse—
Not one board answers.
Frozen panes stare.

In the House of the Dying

So once again, hearing the tired aunts
whisper together under the kitchen globe,
I turn away; I am not one of them.

At the sink I watch the water cover my hands
in a sheath of light. Upstairs she lies alone
dreaming of autumn nights when her children were born.

On the steps between us grows in a hush of waiting
the impossible silence between two generations.
The aunts buzz on like flies around a bulb.

I am dressed like them. Standing with my back turned
I wash the dishes in the same easy way.
Only at birth and death do I utterly fail.

For death is my old friend who waits on the stairs.
Whenever I pass I nod to him like the newsman
who is there every day; for them he is the priest.

While the birth of love is so terrible to me
I feel unworthy of the commonest marriage.
Upstairs she lies, washed through by the two miracles.

My Young Mother

My young mother, her face narrow
and dark with unresolved wishes
under a hatbrim of the twenties,
stood by my middleaged bed.

Still as a child pretending sleep
to a grownup watchful or calling,
I lay in a corner of my dream
staring at the mole above her lip.

Familiar mole! but that girlish look
as if I had nothing to give her—
Eyes blue—brim dark—
calling me from sleep after decades.

The Figure on the Far Side

Once it was my brother on
the far side of the chessboard.
His lean ribcage puffed with
concentration, his lower
lip clenched in his huge second
teeth, he whistled slightly; he
let out his breath as he pounced.

And I was so stupid that
twisting with discomfort I
answered Capablanca's
fifteen-minute pauses with
tears! arias! any old pawn
rushed out in a fury to
die and get the game over!

I must be the only one
alive, I start, who gave up
chess at seven. . . . But the
young doctor waits. What if he
laughs? Shouldn't he care? Damn you,
the silence ticks, how can you
nurse such secrets and keep still?

Iron

Every morning I wake
with blood on my pillow
and the taste of fresh blood
like iron against my tongue.

They say my gums are inflamed
and the bleeding will cease
at first frost—
Each morning the sun wakes me.

I think some nerve is exposed—
it is only August—
or a fine skin was peeled off
the night you were killed.

Conversations at breakfast
have the stripped truth of poems.
All day I wait
for a miraculous letter.

In fact my whole life
leans forward slightly, waiting.
Each day lurches downhill
to its red undoing.

All the Leaves Were Green

Darling, I had my hand on your khaki
knee, the air was shining, the murmur
of small summer grass and insects came in
through the car window. You were saying,
no, singing that theme from Bach, "hung up"
on its repetitions, smiling, unfaltering.
Then was it me beside you in the dark wet
Virginia night when, a curve missed, the wall
smashed into your windshield? O was it me
you saved with a last wrench of will, your hand
white and square on the wheel, my childish
mouth open and screaming?

Letters

1

That quiet point of light
trembled and went out.

Iron touches a log:
it crumbles to coal, then ashes.

The log sleeps in its shape.
A new moon rises.

Darling, my white body
still bears your imprint.

2

Wind chewed at the screen,
rain clawed the window.

Outside three crows
make their harsh, rainy scraping.

Autumn has come
in early July.

On the ground white petals:
my rain-soaked letters.

The Weather of Six Mornings

I

Sunlight lies along my table
like abandoned pages.

I try to speak
of what is so hard for me

—this clutter of a life—
Puritanical signature!

In the prolonged heat insects,
pine needles, birch leaves

make a ground bass of silence
that never quite dies.

2

Treetops are shuddering
in uneasy clusters

like rocking water
whirlpooled before a storm.

Words knock at my breast,
heave and struggle to get out.

A black-capped bird
pecks on, unafraid.

Yield then, yield
to the invading rustle of the rain!

3

All is closed in
by an air so rain-drenched

the distant barking of tied-up dogs
ripples to the heart of the woods.

Only a man's voice
refuses to be absorbed.

Hearing of your death
by a distant roadside

I wanted to erect some marker
though your ashes float out to sea.

4

If the weather breaks
I can speak of your dying,

if the weather breaks,
if the crows stop calling

and flying low
(again today there is thunder, out-

lying . . .),
I can speak of your living,

the lightning-flash of meeting,
the green leaves waving at our windows.

5

Yesterday a letter
spoke of our parting—

a kind of dissolution
so unlike this sudden stoppage.

Now all the years in between
flutter away like lost poems.

And the morning light is so delicate,
so utterly empty. . . .

at high altitude, after long illness,
breathing in mote by mote a vanished world. . . .

6

Rest.
A violin bow, a breeze

just touches the birches.
Cheep—a new flute

tunes up in a birch top.
A chipmunk's warning skirrs. . . .

Whose foot disturbs these twigs?
To the sea of received silence

why should I sign
my name?

March

1. Feathers

I've died, but you are still living!
The pines are still living, and the eastern sky.
Today a great bustle rocks the treetops
of snow and sunshine, dry branches, green brooms.

The pines are cleaning their attics.
Mercilessly, they lop off weak twigs.
If I look down from my window
I can see one of the walks we used to take together.

The snow is covered with brown feathers.
In the fields it's as if an army had just limped by
leaving its slight corpses, abandoned weapons—
a wreckage that will melt into spring.

Nearby is a little grove; on brown needles
we lay side by side telling each other stories.
Against the glass here, listen—
Nothing can stop the huzzah of the male wind!

2. Hunger Moon

The last full moon of February
stalks the fields; barbed wire casts a shadow.
Rising slowly, a beam moved toward the west
stealthily changing position

until now, in the small hours, across the snow
it advances on my pillow
to wake me, not rudely like the sun
but with the cocked gun of silence.

I am alone in a vast room
where a vain woman once slept.
The moon, in pale buckskins, crouches
on guard beside her bed.

Slowly the light wanes, the snow will melt
and all the fences thrum in the spring breeze
but not until that sleeper, trapped
in my body, turns and turns.

3. El Sueño de la Razón

for C. in a mental hospital

Cousin, it's of you I always dream
as I walk these dislocated lawns
or compose a stanza under the Corot trees.

The music of my walking reconciles
somewhat the clipped but common ground
with the lost treetops' thunderous heads.

How they are always muttering in the still
afternoon, how they create
their own darkness under hottest sun.

They compose clouds or a sea
so far above us we can scarcely tell
why such a premonition brushes our cheeks.

Yet as I walk I scan
the woods for a girl's white figure
slipping away among the pines' thin shafts.

Hiding, she is hiding, and in your dreams
the poem's cleared spaces
barely hold out against

marching trees, this suddenly Turner sky.
Poor furious girl, our voices sound
alike (your nurse told me), discreet and gentle.

4. BACK

I was prepared for places
as someone packs bags against hell,
braced to meet each jolt of memory
before I stumbled over it.

Secretly I rehearsed the stages
of our coming to know one another,
furnished each scene with trees,
even a phoebe calling.

So I preserved a wintry face
as I returned little by little
to the rooms where we slept, the closet
where you hung your worn raincoat.

But tonight it's all sham—
From her curtained alcove a woman
hums that aria of Purcell's
negligently, sweetly:

Dido is pleading, Aeneas
blurs into her past, his future.
Again your eyes star
with salt as I choose my elegy.

5. NO MORE ELEGIES

Everyone rushed into town
right after coffee, though the icy ruts
are gray as iron, and icicles
two feet long scarcely drip.

The sun is so bright on the snow
I'm out tramping in dark beach glasses.
A clump of leafless birches
steams against a dark blue sky.

Over there the yellow frame
of some new construction glints,
while the tips of those bushes are bloody
as if tomorrow, tomorrow would be Easter!

And a phoebe is calling, calling.
All the small birds come fluting from the pines:
No more elegies! no more elegies! Poor
fools—it's not even spring.

6. In Silence Where We Breathe

As a boy he was so silent
she raged like a gnat. Summer nights—

Summer nights he stood at his desk
wrapped in a wordless soprano.

Once he constructed a clipper ship
to scale from the *Century Dictionary*.

All May they ran barefoot
through the stinging southern streets.

The air was like mercury,
a heavy silver ball.

And the river stank of salt
and rotten magnolia candles

down the end of the block—Slot machines!
From their grandmother's veranda

she could hear the ring of life
start out through a swing door—

No one could tell such stories;
but he never cried, not once.

7. MIDDLE AGE

At last it's still—a gray thaw.
Who ever saw a more sullen day?
On the porch, among patches of standing water,
a bluejay pecks at an uncovered seed.

It's not even raining. In the vanished night
a brief snow fell, dampening the paths.
The paths are brown with ashes—
or is it the first earth showing through?

The pines are like saints. I'm waiting—
oh, for some insight, some musical phrase,
for the voices of my friends,
for faint traffic noises from the far-off city,

for choruses, for a symphony orchestra,
for the screech of a subway train rounding a bend,
a baby's *ah-ah-ah*
or the rich, hesitant speech of students—

How amazing to be born! A few drops
of rain fling their stones into puddles,
and circles of light ride out
smashing the icy islands—

I can't hear their splash. I'm alert
only to dreams as the rain falls louder.
Each word, each solitude cracks open.
Only the miracle is real.

8. Coda

An air of departures. Silences.
Again the pines are sheathed in a wet snow.
The chimney breathes its slow, transparent smoke.

Everything has been offered, nothing given.
Everything, not the first thing has been said.
After me who will sit here, patiently writing?

Words over a page: a slow smoke
scrolling across the sky what is unconsumed
by the deep, thunderous fires of the house—

An air of departures. Now the tall city
stoops to receive us, where we blur like snow
leaving behind a breath of loves and angers.

Maps & Windows

(1974)

I

Mercator's World:

Poems

1947–1951

Mercator, *1512–94. Flemish geographer, mathematician, and cartographer. . . . In 1568 appeared his first map using the projection which has since borne his name and which has been more generally used than any other projection for navigators' maps of the world.*

Mercator's projection *is of great value to navigators, since it shows true directions, but it has great disadvantages for general use. The parallels and meridians are represented as straight lines, intersecting at right angles. The length of a degree of latitude is thus represented as the same in higher latitudes as it is at the equator. To preserve the correct proportion between a degree of longitude and a degree of latitude, the length of a degree of longitude must be correspondingly increased, and the result is a misrepresentation of areas and distances, increasing with distance from the equator. In a* MAP *on Mercator's projection, Greenland appears larger than South America, and Alaska comparable in size with the United States. . . . Of course, also, it is impossible to represent at all the areas very near the poles.*

—THE COLUMBIA ENCYCLOPEDIA (1945)

Eve

Now she is still not beautiful but more
Moving than before, for time has come
When she shall be delivered; some-
one must have, move her, or the doors
Be shuttered over, the doorlids shut, her
Eyes' lies shattered. In the spume
Of a triple wave she lives: sperm,
Man and life's mate break like flags upon her shore.

Marriage must take her now, or the sly
Inquirer, inviting her to ship for his sake,
Will share all islands inland with her, her sky
No one else shares, will slake
Conquerlust. Seas wash away her ties
While through her thigh-trees water strikes like a snake.

For a Boy Born in Wartime

Head first, face down, into Mercator's world
Like an ungainly rocket the child comes,
Driving dead-reckoned outward through a channel
Where nine months back breath was determined
By love, leaving his watery pen
—That concrete womb with its round concrete walls
Which he could make a globe of all his own—
For flatter, dryer enemies, for home.

Boy we have set in motion like an engine,
Bound by our instruments no one knows where
Until upending you are zero London,
Headlong from water, what will you make of air?
An empire? light to whistle through? a ball
To bounce? Or will your tumbling feet
Drop down and inward to the concrete
Unmalleable mirror world we live in,

Inheritor of our geographies,
Just as we rise to slap your fluttering cry?

P.O.W.

Suffering sets us apart. We enjoy too strongly.
For the ex-P.O.W. New York sparkles with anguish,
A skyline of cakes and lights and too many nude
Women. Every loaf of bread rips his throat like a lash,
And the scars of these lashes separate him more strangely
From his fellows than visible scars or his years without food.

He moves through New York like a man off an operating table,
A tangible silence around him, an ether cone,
While American tastes and words in his mouth glitter
Like knocked-out teeth. Their power alone,
Their value, *English,* is such that he is unable
To string a sentence with them. He might shatter
Memory, joy, guilt—his bell of glass
Which keeps even the girls he kisses from touching his face.

The Door

Intelligent companion,
Talented—yes, and blind—but can
I live the pitiful part I play?
For what do you see when I
Come to you? Isn't it woman,
Passion, a pair of eyes, the ground
To prove old sex and sorrows on?
Tomorrow, if you were blinded
Really, physically, could you
Picture me as I come through
This door? Could you construct a me,
All physical reality,
And then, easy as light,
Penetrate the lips I speak from,
Plant them with speech or start
Thought with your kisses?
                                        I am
A person after all. You are
A person. We are proud and fear
The same things: pride of possession,
Cowardice, communication
Stopped.
                    Silhouetted in this door
I stop a moment like a stranger
Before the darkness. What do you see?
I wait for eyes, then tongues to join,
Intelligent, companions.

a poem with capital letters

john berryman asked me to write a poem about roosters.
elizabeth bishop, he said, once wrote a poem about roosters.
do your poems use capital letters? he asked.   *like god?*
i said.   *god no,* he said, *like princeton!*   i said,
god preserve me if i ever write a poem about princeton, and i thought,
o john berryman, what has brought me into this company of poets
where the masculine thing to do is use capital letters
and even princeton struts like one of god's betters?

Song

Here I am yours, and here, and here:
In body, wit and in responsibility.
And here I am not yours: inquire
Of my first lover for my fire
And of my second for my subtlety.

In the menagerie of thought
You own the elephant but not the man,
But since humanity grew out
Of the same cell, of the same root,
Why do you cry? You suck the larger crumb.

Move through the larger rooms, explore
The earliest if not the dark, dark continents;
And what you have I had before
Either my subtlety or fire:
Brutal before Biblical innocence.

The Urge To Tell the Truth

The urge to tell the truth
Strips sensuality
Like bark stripped from a tree.
Bone-nakedness and growth
Are incompatible;
The stripped tree falls.

After the squirrels finish,
The white squirrels of the brain,
Such naturalness is driven
From the body's wish,
Such diffidence and humor,
That a white score

Of toothmarks at the root
Of unity is all
The tree surgeon reveals,
Past mending with concrete;
And sycamore and oak
And marriage break.

Twins

You ask for love but what you want is healing,
Selfishly, understandably. You pray
For marriage as another man might pray
For sleep after surgery, failing
More ether, miraculous cure by a saint
Or the tissues still uncut. You want
Never again to look at incompleteness,
Yours or mine or ours; this is our weakness.

All the images you use are of darkness—
Sleep, forgiveness, physical unity
Transcending daylight bodies and the rays
Where a Curie works or wounded priests confess.
You won't believe you're maimed, you won't believe
There is any other way to live
Than whole. You're as careful of your honor
As any cripple; this is our humor.

But I'm ashamed—shamed by the doctors
You've prayed to in the hope someone might close
Your eyes in passion, shamed that I expose
And kill and heal you with the simplest finger.
I'm radium, apocalypse in the breast;
I understand—this is my selfishness.
And while love dies cancered by light, I
Hesitate and can neither live nor die.

The Knowledge That Comes
Through Experience

I feel my face being bitten by the tides
Of knowledge as sea-tides bite at a beach;
Love leaves its implications, wars encroach
On the flat white square between my ear and jaw
Picking it as the sea hollows out sand. . . .
I might as well stick my head in the maw

Of the ocean as live this generously:
Feelings aside I never know my face;
I comb my hair and what I see is timeless,
Not a face at all but (besides the hair)
Lips and a pair of eyes, two hands, a body
Pale as a fish imprisoned in the mirror.

When shall I rest, when shall I find myself
The way I'll be, iced in a shop window?
Maybe I'll wake tonight in the undertow
Of sleep and lie adrift, gutted helpless
By the salt at my blue eyes—then the gulfs
Of looks and desire will shine clean at last.

Meanwhile I use myself. I am useful
Rather foolishly, like a fish who yearns
Dimly toward daylight. There is much to learn
And curiosity riddles our rewards.
It seems to me I may be capable,
Once I'm a skeleton, of love and wars.

Long View from the Suburbs

Yes, I'm the lady he wrote the sonnets to.
I can tell you how it was
And where the books lie, biographies and his
Famous later versions now collected
In one volume for lovers. (You
Can never really analyze his method

If you only read those.) Once for instance
He begged to meet me under an oak
Outside the city after five o'clock.
It was early April. I waited there
Until in the distance
A streetlight yielded to the sensual air

Then I walked home again. The next day
He was touchy and elated
Because of a new poem which he said
Marked some advance—perhaps that "honest" style
Which prostitutes our memories.
He gave it to me. I said nothing at all

Being weary. It had happened so often.
He was always deluding himself
Complaining (honestly) that I spurned his gifts.
Shall I tell you what gifts are? Although I said
Nothing at the time
I still remember evenings when I learned

The tricks of style. Do you know, young man,
Do they teach you in biographies
How it feels to open like a city
At the caress of darkness, then sickening
To walk about alone
Until a streetlamp yawns in reckoning?

After the Bomb Tests

1

The atom bellies like a cauliflower,
Expands, expands, shoots up again, expands
Into ecclesiastical curves and towers
We pray to with our cupped and empty hands.
This is the old Hebraic-featured fear
We nursed before humility began,
Our crown-on-crown or phallic parody
Begat by man on the original sea.

The sea's delivered. Galvanized and smooth
She kills a tired ship left in her lap
—Transfiguration—with a half-breath
Settling like an animal in sleep.
So godhead takes the difficult form of love.
Where is the little myth we used to have?

2

Where is the simple myth we used to have?
The childish mother and her fatherless son,
That infinitesimal act, creation,
Which shocks two cells so that they melt and solve
A riddle of light and all our darkness tears
With meanings like struck water round a stone?
Is it all gone? Are the meanings gone?

I walk out of the house into the still air,
Moving from circle to circle—hot, cold,
Like zones of water this October night.
All the stars are still arranged in spheres,

The planets stalk serenely. Thinking of Kepler
I pick a grassblade, chew it up, then spit.
Now I have thought, he said, *the thoughts of God.*

      3

Now I have thought the very thoughts of God!
Mentally checking the sky he doused his lamp
And let the worlds come to life inside him.
And if he were wrong? Could one harmony hold
The sum of private freedoms like a cup?
He glanced outward. Affectionately, delicately.
Distance received him in a lap of sleep;
He felt its warm muzzle on his eye.
He smiled, darkening. He had caged the sky.

When he woke up dawn stretched like a canvas,
Empty and deep. Over the slick seal river
A wind skated. Kepler, curious, rose,
Started to cross himself—then like a lover
Or virgin artist gave himself to his power.

In a Room with Picassos

Draw as you will there are no images
Which exactly reproduce this state of mind!
No bull can satisfy my unspoken anger
Or Spanish boys speak plainly for my love
While you refuse it. I can stand and stand
In front of canvas and artistic paraphernalia
But nothing there will answer me with pride:
I am the exact shade of shame and desire.
Your justification in the face of his
Simple indifference to simple fire.
I am the offering which always moves
Anyone, no matter how far away he is from love.

Gaza

Too calm to beg for pity yet too strained
Ever to call my bluff or disown me
Openly, you said nothing but remained
Masterful—I thought weak—solitary,
Like one of those old kings without a face
Who flank in tiers of weatherbeaten stone
The O of a cathedral carapace:
Unmouthed, you groped like Samson to be dethroned.

Meteors

Whom can we love in all these little wars?
The aviator, king of his maps and glowing lights
But dispossessed of six-foot-two of ground?
The sailor, blind as a worm, suspended
In a hammock made of scrap iron, in his fear
Heavy and liquid to the touch as night?

Whom can we love? The same question
Asked five years back drops through my ear and dies
With a fizzle of brightness at the center of my brain.
The sky is streaked with pilots falling. I see
Buried in altitude like meteors
Cartoons of wit and sex, skeletons of leaders.

A Bedside Rune

Not jealousy but pale disgust complains:
So here's what all those gentle manners come to!
Meaning ourselves, meaning the three years' passion
We've watched over like a sick child

All day and night. Only last night I sat
Waiting for a heartbeat like an old woman
Rocking away. Death-*life* her rockers say.
Life-*death* sighed the small heartbeat.

Obligations

Here where we are, wrapped in the afternoon
As in a chrysalis of silken light,
Our bodies kindly holding one another
Against the press of vision from outside,
Here where we clasp in a stubble field
Is all the safety either of us hopes for,
Stubbornly constructing walls of night
Out of the ordered energies of the sun.

With the same gratitude I feel the hot
Dazzle on my eyelids and your hand
Carefully opening my shaded breasts.
The air is very high and still. The buzz
And tickle of an insect glow and fuse
Into the flicker of a pulse. We rest
Closed in the golden shallows of a sound.
Once, opening my eyes, I surprise your trust.

My fingers pick at a broken shining blade
Of stubble as you bend to look at me.
What can I do to help you? What extreme
Unction after love is laid upon us?
The act itself has built this sphere of anguish
Which we must now inhabit like our dreams,
The dark home of our polarities
And our defense, which we cannot evade.

2

Nothing Has Been

Used in the

Manufacture of

This Poetry

That Could Have

Been Used in the

Manufacture of

Bread

A long time ago I had a student who was married to a tugboat captain. She had three babies and used to get up at five in the morning to work on her stories before the children woke. The reasons why she was finding it hard to do the writing that was in her were not far to seek, yet she and her husband, who were Catholic, expected a still larger family. I have no idea what happened to that young woman; perhaps she is back at the typewriter now, with the last child in school. But more than two decades of teaching women—talented, intellectually curious and passionately eager to live their lives—have convinced me she's not an isolated example. Tillie Olsen, in particular, has written movingly of the "Silences When Writers Don't Write," of women's silences, and at the same time of her own desire to cry out at H. H. Richardson ("There are enough women to do the childbearing and childrearing. I know of none who can write my books."): "Yes, and I know of none who can bear and rear my children either!"

Women, surely, have always written—just as in preliterate times they must have been storytellers and weavers of legends alongside men. But if this is true, why did so many stop? Or, if they kept on, why have so few published? Such questions are very much in the air right now, and the commonest answer, following Olsen, is that marriage along the old, accepted lines and, especially, childbearing and childrearing can sap energy, privacy, a sense of the earned right to write. The last invasion may well be the most serious one. "Them lady poets must not marry, pal," declares John Berryman's Henry, suggesting also—oh, but don't we all recognize what he suggests?

I've never married, have no children, so you could say my case was always different. Yet from the age of twenty-two to the age of twenty-six, I worked strenuously and perfectly seriously on a book of poems (a *book,* not just poems), then "gave up poetry" and never tried to publish but one of them. Why? Does this mean the same injunctions have affected all women, not just the wives and mothers? Haven't we been most deeply shaped in our very expectations of ourselves, and isn't this what has been most daunting? In fact, since I was unmarried and belonged to a marrying generation, was I in a special way vulnerable to the unspoken words: "What sort of woman are you?"

While I was working on my book, I told people I didn't believe in magazine publication because all my poems were related. Privately, I felt the poems were never finished. I suspect most privately of all, I couldn't face living out the full range of intuition they revealed. Later, after I'd come back to writing and was beginning to publish in magazines and an occasional anthology, the old poems still seemed to throw off balance whatever I was currently doing. After 1956 or so, I only remember looking at them once until recently. For a while I believed I'd destroyed them. They turned up on a lower shelf of my bookcase, in an old Christmas card box, along with drafts and drafts of later and often less striking work.

In the winter of 1971–72, friends looking at some new manuscripts of mine claimed that I was changing. The new poems seemed more tense, more aggressive than those in my first collection, *The Weather of Six Mornings,* written mostly during my thirties and finally published in 1969. And it's true that book is full of acceptances, apparently traditional but hard won. Above all the self is seen as no more important than anybody else, a self in a world of selves who give one another strength and life. (One poem, for my mother, ends "Which one of us is absent?" The book ends "why should I sign / my name?") I said no, I thought I was just getting back to something closer to the mood of my earliest work. Earliest work? I hesitated, made excuses, but before long the living-room floor was carpeted with dozens of old yellow scratch sheets.

Now I was the one to be surprised. For one thing, there were many more poems than I'd imagined: eighty-odd in all. Then, there were some good, complete poems I had no recollection of writing. It was a shock to discover that at some point, probably in the mid-fifties, I'd thought enough of the poems to go through and date a number of them; also that where various drafts existed, I'd as often as not made a poem less rather than more interesting. Some poems got angrier and sharper and less abstract as they went along, but others lost their initial honesty and became over-complicated. This was particularly true of poems which I'd tried to rewrite between 1952 and 1954, after the impulse toward that first collection was spent. Finally, it was a shock to find that I'd forgotten, or distorted, or perhaps never truly faced what the book was "about."

What I Had Told Myself

What I had told myself, what I remember telling myself in my twenties, was that I was writing a book of war poems from a civilian's, a woman's, point of view. World War II was the war I grew up into. I was fourteen when England and France declared war on Germany (and I came from a fiercely internationally minded, interventionist family, except that my brother, just older than myself, was for a short time a pacifist); I was seventeen at the time of Pearl Harbor; the first atomic bombs were dropped on Hiroshima and Nagasaki, and peace treaties were signed, just before my senior year in college. From 1946 to 1950, those intense writing years, I lived in Princeton, which was full of returned veterans studying on the G.I. Bill. I was even an associate member of a veterans' group which met to discuss issues like the implementation of the Marshall Plan. In the summer of 1947 I went to England and France before it was possible for an American to do so without a reason recognized by the host government. I went to study at the first Oxford summer school, along with many students and professors from the great pre-war universities of Europe. These men and women, in their heavy sandals and worn, stained shirt collars, I found in a state of euphoria because they could talk to one another for the first time in eight years. London was still full of bombed-out sites being converted into car parks, except that there were few cars. Wherever I walked a single hammer could be heard tapping. In late August I crossed the Channel. At Boulogne the only solid things left in the landscape were the German fortifications and submarine pens, with here and there a foundered Allied invasion ship. Elsewhere along the

French coast the V-2 rocket pens still humped up like molehills made of cement. In Paris I saw a sign in a department-store window that read, over a display of wicker furniture: NOTHING HAS BEEN USED IN THE MANUFACTURE OF THIS FURNITURE THAT COULD HAVE BEEN USED IN THE MANUFACTURE OF BREAD.

How everything looked, what the European professors said, changed my life, quite simply. I find I wrote home in the middle of that summer: "I woke the other morning with the realization that I should have to write, and probably write poetry. This made me feel foolish, more than anything else. I distrust poets, and have been fighting the idea for about five years now. Just as I have been fighting the idea of teaching. But perhaps they are both necessary."

At Oxford our tutors were members of the Oxford Extra-Mural Delegacy, which during the winters sent men and women into rural villages to conduct workers' education courses in literature, history, social philosophy, that were to run for four consecutive years. This project had the blessing of the post-Churchill Labour Government. It was a kind of teaching I had never really imagined, despite having graduated from a midwestern state university which had a whole campus dedicated to agronomy, for the sake of its constituent farmers, and ran "short courses" in cheese-making. At Oxford also our tutors read poetry aloud to us in the evenings, something that rarely happened in those days in the United States; readings, like chamber music, had been popular in the bomb shelters, the Underground stations, during the London blitz. The European professors never tired of quoting poems to one another in Czech, Russian or Polish, French. For the first time poetry presented itself to me as a means of survival.

So I came home in September not to start to write (for I had written poems all during high school and had recently begun again after a long wartime silence) but with a focus. This war had been, I thought, peculiarly a civilians' war, the war of the bombed-out cities and of ruined, isolated country houses in northern France. Even now, two years later, the dark bread, made of potatoes or sometimes even sawdust, flattened almost to the tabletop when you pressed it with a sharp knife.

I thought, at the same time, that all wars are probably total for the people living through them; the Hundred Years' War must have been a total civilians' war. For civilians, read women—women-and-children, women-and-the-sick-and-the-old. Yet of course, women had not just been civilians during World War II, not just the passive receivers of suffering. At Oxford I knew a young Frenchwoman who had been a member of the Resistance; my best English friend was just out of the WRENS, the women's branch of the Royal Navy. I had myself spent several terms at college studying to be a meteorologist—astronomy, navigation, physics—with the difference that I hadn't really needed to, in America where women were never drafted, and after a while I had switched to languages, with some vague idea (since I imagined the war would go on and on) of a translating job in Washington.

I would write as a noncombatant, a witness. It was the air war I was most haunted by, since my brother, my father, my uncle, my brother-in-law had all been involved in aviation in some form during the war years. I never could get over the peculiar beauty of a bombed-out landscape (which needless to say I only saw once the worst had been cleaned up, once the summer field flowers—poppies and fireweed and ragwort—had seeded themselves and started blooming over the rubble); nor my guilt because I found the desolation visually beautiful. I had two friends from childhood, now returned veterans, who had been shot down as pilots over Europe and imprisoned; one later made his way to Ravensbruck and helped repatriate French survivors of the concentration camp there. I hated the very idea of war, all its details, yet obviously, I was excited and absorbed by it, and also I felt guilty because I had not participated in any direct way, only through association. And how could you write except from experience?

Perhaps, as Grace Paley has suggested, this was one of the true problems of women writers at that time. The men's lives seemed more central than ours, almost more truthful. They had been shot down, or squirmed up the beaches. We had waited for their letters. Again, I was not a European or an Englishwoman. Yet when I hesitated to comment on Dylan Thomas's "A Refusal to Mourn the Death, by Fire, of a Child in London," then quite a new poem, in my Oxford seminar, because I had not lived through the blitz, my tutor said soberly, "Thank God you were spared that."

And even now I have to ask myself: Why did I feel the need to write about the holocaust almost more than individual human relations, or to disguise my purpose to myself? What fascination with the will, as well as sympathy, did that reflect?

Hearing poems read aloud in the long, light Oxford evenings brought not only Thomas but, even more vividly, Hopkins and Yeats alive for me. Was it for this reason, I wonder, that all the poets I turned to when I started to write again were neither Americans nor women? What would have happened if I'd listened to William Carlos Williams instead, with his love for casual American speech rhythms, or if I'd valued Emily Dickinson more? Auden was out of favor in England when I was there, because after serving as a model of political engagement during the thirties, he had come to the United States just before the outbreak of World War II, thus escaping much of what he had helped others prepare their minds for. A cop-out, it seemed to the young tutors, who stubbornly read us Day Lewis and MacNeice instead. But I'd long been familiar with the work of Auden and also Spender, and when I thought of a contemporary, politically aware tone of voice, that was the tone I still thought in. Because of my work in languages, I was also steeped in the poetry of García Lorca, with its mixture of surrealism and people's theater, but it was only much later that I could begin to understand what that combination might mean to me.

"A BOOK OF WAR POEMS"

Had I published my book of poems in 1950 or '51 or '52, as I suppose could have happened, it would certainly not have been the same collection I now call *Mercator's World*. It would have been longer, rougher and more mixed in tone, and it would have contained many more political poems. It would have been more like (though still not clearly) "a book of war poems from a woman's point of view." For especially to begin with, war and its survivors made up much of my conscious subject matter; and even my imagery (which is not, as Adrienne Rich has pointed out, a product of our conscious choice so much as it is something thrown up on our consciousness, like our dreams) was dominated by explosions, mapmaking and stars and navigation, and scientific discovery. I was writing with a curious amalgam of seventeenth-century and twentieth-century references. Behind the American atomic-bomb tests in the Pacific in 1946, I perceived the *hubris* of Kepler (nevertheless a genuinely religious man), and the fact that the first silk I saw after five years of wartime was a parachutist's landing chart, made into a woman's headscarf, somehow got mixed up in my mind with my father's collection of early European maps of the discovery and colonization of Florida. Most of these maps were based on Mercator's projection, with its squared-off yet strangely exaggerated perspectives. If "Mercator's world" was in an obvious sense my father's world, it also suggested a habit of thinking which, distorted and then followed down to its logical end (as Einstein's theory prepared the way for the hydrogen bomb, which Einstein protested), had plunged us into global conflict for the second time in a generation.

Not that my imagery was only a kind of large abstract grid taken from warmaking and the physics of fission and light. There are also specific human images in many of the early poems that still have the power to take me a bit by surprise and so to move me.

> In bomb shelters many are honest
> As Jews are
> Pierced by the knowledge of bullets in bullet-proof cars.

was written even before I went abroad. Until I came on a line about German children holding out their palms to beg as a closed train blurs by, I'd forgotten that civilian trains were still sealed in the Occupied Zones in 1947. And an ex-P.O.W. reentering New York

> ... like a man off an operating table
> A tangible silence around him, an ether cone.
> While American tastes and words in his mouth glitter
> Like knocked-out teeth ...

is dazed by his own inarticulateness: "his bell of glass / Which keeps even the girls he kisses from touching his face."

Perhaps it is important that these poems were begun in a climate which, while it countenanced—with a good deal of protest—the Bikini bomb tests, also saw the making of the United Nations, the Marshall Plan and other schemes for the reconstruction of Europe, and not long afterward the first Fulbright scholarships. And although the reasons were certainly more personal than political, I wonder if it is wholly irrelevant that the poems ended, trickled away, at about the point when the McCarthy hearings became possible?

Now that we turn against the whole notion that the United States should be a moral leader in world affairs—as if we could tell others what to feel and how to govern themselves—it's hard to remember the optimism and seriousness of the first couple of years after the end of World War II, when many people, including many returned veterans, felt responsible for rebuilding Europe and Japan physically and economically and, above all, for restoring communications among nations. I think some of that optimism got into my poems, at least in the form of a confidence that I could write them. Several are positive statements of international responsibility. At the same time, there is some hopelessness that we (that is, Americans), or at least I myself, could ever rise above the fact that our experiences had *not* been those of the damaged civilian populations:

> For past a certain knowledge
> Of headlines there can be no sharing. . . .

> And Europe's children cease to live
> For a moment in our minds

And a certain bombed corner kind-
ly obliterates itself. . . .

It was a celebration of spring, that poem!

Another poem asks what happens to peasants in a war ("Women
go / On sweeping out the house where they were killed"), while ex-
ploring the state of mind of the wisest human beings, which I saw as a
kind of recovered innocence, knowledge tempered by extremes of
mental and physical suffering. I couldn't forget the two Czech profes-
sors in my Oxford seminar who, even in 1947, no longer looked for-
ward to political freedom but used to argue endlessly over how, under
totalitarian conditions, one could preserve freedom of the spirit. I con-
cluded that "Universal concern is not enough." "The great gas cham-
bers of the mind shut down" on whatever we fail to accomplish in our
own persons. Struggling to define my own religious consciousness be-
tween the poles of Christianity and Existentialism, I prayed, "Why,
while cities burn, do I still live?"

> I have no faith, I do not expect to recover
> Any but myself, the unit, man.
> Mass charity affects me like an ether
> Empty of consciousness as of its pain.

The Archipelago of Love

"Not enough scherzi," said my brother affectionately, when my 1969
book came out, and indeed I consider it a great weakness in my writ-
ing that I'm so shy about dealing with joy. For I've known real joys in
my life, and the period I'm talking about was unusually full of them.
The war, though it obsessed me, was over. Horizons were expanding
not only geographically and politically but personally for me. The men
were back. I was living in a men's university town. When I think of the
year 1948, I can hardly remember times when I was alone (though

there must have been some, while I worked on my poems or finished another half-day's stint of freelance editing). What I remember instead is tramping across fields or driving in an open car with one companion or another; climbing the scaffolding of some new postwar housing because I was excited about architecture; sitting in on seminars on literature or philosophy and then talking afterward under a dogwood tree or hunched over bowls of homemade soup at a student restaurant. Or, later, when it seemed as if some kind of decision must be drawing near, there were the evenings of mutual silence and intense, diffident questionings.

Marriage was on everybody's mind in those days, men's as well as women's, after the fragmentation of the war, and most of my friends wanted three or four babies as soon as they could afford them. For the veterans studying on the G.I. Bill, there was a rush to put down roots, to "get started." Still, it was curiously difficult, if you hadn't married during the war, to imagine how a peacetime relationship could develop slowly and quietly and reach fruition without the drastic backdrop of wartime leaves, wartime ultimatums. I sometimes wonder if I knew how to make a decision for several years after I stopped reading casualty lists. On the windowsills of the dormitories were large metal stars giving the names of former Princeton students who had occupied rooms there and been killed; often they were names I knew. Yet I used to feel a kind of outrageous triumph, an elation that seemed as if it would grow and grow and might take over everything. I was young, alive, free, learning to know myself and others, learning my craft of poetry, all my senses were opening.

So, no matter what headlines I gave my work, from the first I was exploring other territory: "Look where the archipelago of love / Lies at our feet, the waves washing like fever, / Conscious, unconscious. . . ." The earliest complete poem in this volume, "Eve," written when I was just twenty-three, is a poem of sexual awakening, frankly acknowledged. "In the spume / Of a triple wave she lives: sperm, / Man and life's mate break like flags upon her shore." What can I say now to those images of conquest? At the same time the sexual overview ("Marriage must take her now, or . . .") shows how much I was still living within a social pattern, or at least a pattern of expectation, as clearly defined as the physical world had once seemed to be according to Mercator's projection. Out of the tension between that enclosing, conservative order and my own expanding vision and senses came what I later recognized to be the strongest pages of my abandoned "book."

For here, as was not true of the war poems, there could be no question of authenticity. Despite the limitations on sexual roles which the poems alternately question and confirm, relationships between women and men are seen in individual terms and, increasingly, with unsparing eyes. It was in 1948 that I wrote "The Door" (other versions speak of "this double door"), which is a plea for equality and for not being treated as a sexual object. While this poem seems simply honest today, I wonder how it would have sounded had it been published at the time? Interestingly, I wasn't really able to deal with all it said myself. The draft I finally settled on cut out the lines "I am / A person after all, you are / A person . . ." and substituted at the end a vision of almost supernatural union. Having asked the man not to be a god, did I get scared? Somehow I was trying, in imagination, to revive some perfect model of the trap I needed to spring.

Perhaps not surprisingly, poems that promised most in the way of love and growth were often distanced by their forms. This too was part of the world, social and literary, that surrounded me. Probably it was also part of my own mind-set. "Eve" is modeled on sonnets by Hopkins. I wrote a lot of songs, following seventeenth-century examples as well as Yeats and Auden. These stay with me now mainly for what they reveal in spite of, not because of, their manners. "I guard my independence / Which beautifully guards / Me . . ." seems chilling in its implications. More sympathetic is a song written for a friend on his thirtieth birthday, though again, I can't help speculating on what it might have meant to other women had it come out when it was composed:

En l'an trentiesme de mon aage
Perhaps I shall be wiser,
More certain than I am here
In the coils of my heritage.

Que toutes mes hontes j'eus bues—
At twenty-three
I am caught in such necessity
To be a man, the crowd's hero,

Que toutes mes hontes j'eus bues.
I would be double,
Half lover-poet-sybil,
Half what the kind nets swallow. . . .

Did I want to be a man? Not that I can remember, certainly not sexually. But I must have thought that "To be a man, the crowd's hero" was what becoming a published poet would mean; it was where my ambition was driving me. Then the definition changes to something female but disturbing: "Half lover-poet-sybil." How could you be a sybil by halves? I recognized, though I still did not fully recognize, the doubleness of my urge to become. What was expected of me, what I wanted for myself in the most profound ways, was marriage and children. I saw the "nets" as "kind," even though they were also the "coils" of my middle-class heritage. (And I was still living at home.) I didn't really think you could be double. At the University of Iowa, some years later, a classmate told me he believed that to be a woman poet was "a contradiction in terms." But by then I had gone back to writing, and for keeps.

john berryman asked me to write a poem about roosters.
elizabeth bishop, he said, once wrote a poem about roosters.
do your poems use capital letters? he asked.   *like god?*
i said.   *god no,* he said, *like princeton!*

There is something in this rhyme that even today brings back the rollicking fall afternoon when Berryman, then a young instructor and no more than a campus acquaintance, rushed across the college lawn and, without even pausing to say hello, began to tell me how to write my poems! Not because of what it says (I recorded the conversation almost in its entirety) but because it catches some of the laughter yet also bewilderment I felt at "the company of poets," where "the masculine thing to do," etc.

Princeton truly was a male stronghold in those days, and no doubt this intensified my own sense of a dichotomy between "woman" and "poet." I knew a number of men who wrote but no women. Work by women was still only sparsely represented in contemporary poetry anthologies. Now that I have a number of women friends who are poets, it's hard to recall the particular kind of isolation I felt in my writing or my almost beleaguered self-questioning.

I do remember how, when I was about fourteen, my sister had brought home from Vassar Muriel Rukeyser's first two books and I had a sudden glimpse of a young woman, not much older than my sister, who was out in the world writing poems; it seemed a life of extraordinary courage. I continued to hear about Rukeyser from time to time. Otherwise, men's praise of women poets didn't seem to go much beyond Marianne Moore and Elizabeth Bishop, whose work I admired but couldn't then *use,* in the deep sense that writers use the discoveries of other writers as steps toward their own growth. Somehow I had absorbed out of the New Critical air itself (because I honestly don't remember anyone's telling me so) that women have trouble managing traditional meters with authority and verve and also can't handle long lines. Emily Dickinson's lines were short, and besides, since I knew only the bowdlerized, smoothed-over versions of her poems, it didn't occur to me how original she could be musically within those repeated New England hymn tunes. So I went to school to what models I could find—mostly the British poets already mentioned—to learn long rhythmic periods and metrical invention within the forms. The subjects I was writing about—war and relations between women and men—seemed also mostly to have remained the property of men.

I'm afraid it is typical—the year was still only 1948—that I was at my most "literary" when I wrote a loose theme-and-variations using characters from *The Tempest* as voices for my own deep-seated fears:

> *Prospero:*
> Health is what I have to buy for my children.
> If I ransom grace, that dream of prows and discovery
> And all except a physical creation,
> Do you think I can have it? will the stirrings of the air let me?

> *Miranda:*
> O sweet Ariel, sweet strings who play with the idea of pain
> Not feeling it, who don't take in the cost
> Of following music suffered by the brain
> And not the blood, can't you hear the sailors cry *All's lost!*

That first line was, I know, meant quite literally. I was concerned for my unborn children if I persisted in being a writer, not primarily devoted to "a physical creation." Never very strong, I questioned whether I would have the energy to be a good mother unless I gave up other options.

The second stanza is still more complicated. For the old worry that to write might mean to wait on the sidelines, not really to act and suffer and "exist," which was present in the poems about wartime as guilt at nonparticipation, was now beginning to be metamorphosed into a conflict between writing and my own sexuality. Here, as Miranda follows "music suffered by the brain / And not the blood," it is the "sailors" who cry *All's lost!* In a very early poem I had written "Everyone's childhood lies buried in the sea." Several years later, in the poem "Meteors," I was to make the farseeing, less physical (as I thought then) artist-lover into the "aviator," who suffers only in imagination as he bombs, while the "sailor," the lover who promises sexual and family satisfaction, lies mired in his very physicality. Almost half *Mercator's World,* and in particular the poems of 1949 and 1950, explore, on the one hand, the dilemma of a woman artist in love with a man who is not an artist and who therefore can't altogether share her cravings ("Could you construct a me / All physical reality?") and, on the other hand, the dilemma of one in love with a fellow artist ("I still remember evenings when I learned / The tricks of style . . ."). In a poem finished just before I stopped writing, "In a Room with Picassos," the woman artist is questioning not only the male artist but the tools of her own art, that is, the morality of her creative impulse.

Even that 1947 poem about "the archipelago of love," written out of all my dazzled awareness of the possibilities ahead of me and called "Design for an Odyssey," ends

> But perhaps our gods are weak, those islands useless
>
> Where they lie bright-eyed on the field of our illusion,
> White and flat like a fleet of summer boats.
> Suppose they are really too small and we sail alone
> Past the antipodes of desire and doubt?

QUESTIONS OF AUTOBIOGRAPHY

But poetry isn't autobiography, and if some of the poems I've quoted from here most extensively were more successful, I probably wouldn't use them in the same way. For what poetry must do is alert us to a truth, and it must be necessary; once it exists, we realize how much we needed exactly this. Writing about the war was important for me personally, but I didn't, couldn't have much to say about it that could be fresh for others—as, for instance, Dylan Thomas's "A Refusal to Mourn" and "Holy Spring" had brought me up short when I first read them in the little book *Deaths and Entrances,* standing in a London bookstall, wondering if I could afford to buy. In the end, my book was never "a book of war poems from a woman's point of view," for the reason that the real discoveries I was making in those days were being documented in the poems about man-woman relationships, which nevertheless depended on a lot of the same imagery. The most truthful poem I was to write about World War II—the elegy called "The Faithful"—didn't come along until 1955, ten years after the fact. There the point is not so much the narrator's grief (real enough) as her realization that her "blameless" life has been a kind of not living. I finally wrote my poem about being a nonparticipant, about the guilt of that, and I found after this country had been in Vietnam for almost ten years that the poem took on new meaning and was again just as valid for me, and valid to be read aloud, as it had seemed originally.

A poem uses everything we know, the surprising things we notice, whatever we can't solve that keeps on growing, but it has to reach beyond autobiography even to stay on the page. Autobiography is not true enough; it has to be rearranged to release its full meaning. What I see in the poems that now go under the title "Mercator's World" is a rapid wearing-away of assumptions about what a love relationship should and can be between two people. At the time I was writing some of the later poems, these truths seemed terrible. In an early 1950s journal I find the note: "Perhaps I am afraid to write [because] . . . I might kill some comfortable acceptance of myself in the minds of other people, or even in my own mind." Adrienne Rich has spoken of the need of women writers to be *nice*. The "you" of the poems is a projection of any one of three men (not who they were but the archetypes I made of them), but also, of course, there are poems in which the "you" is imaginary, like "Long View from the Suburbs," where, at least partly, I was trying to invent how it might feel to be the old Maud Gonne, whose extraordinary photographs had appeared in *Life* magazine. The rhetoric remains heavy (that need to write long lines, to have a battery of sound-effects at my command—like a man?), but, at best, the passion speaks through its frames. In cutting eighty-odd poems down to sixteen, in the end I've wanted to keep very few of the "war" poems. In any case, by 1951 the war had begun to seem like a mask, something to write *through* in order to express a desolation that had become personal:

> Guilt, war, disease—pillars of violence
> To keep a roof of symbols over my head.
> Still the rain soaks my bed
> Whenever the wind blows, riddling innocence.
> A few survive
> By the effort of some individual love.

Is this what I thought, that only through some personal commitment could there be any real survival? By then, or anyway by a year later, with a record of three failed attempts at relationship inside five years, my chances must have seemed pretty slim.

WHY DIDN'T I PUBLISH?

Why, then, didn't I publish? And why, even more, did I give up writing poems, and when I went back to poems eventually change my style, after I'd worked so hard to make myself into a certain kind of poet during five crucially formative years? In fact, by the winter of 1951–52, it felt almost more as if poetry had given me up.

I think it is important to ask these questions just because I didn't give up poetry for marriage, or to have a baby, or because the family washing was getting hopelessly ahead of me. Maybe I gave it up, or put it to one side, precisely because I still hoped for those things. If this seems cowardly: "Didn't anyone ever tell you it was all right to write?" asked the psychiatrist who came along much later. "Yes, but not to be a writer." Behind me lay the sort of upper-middle-class education that encourages writing, painting, music, theater so long as they aren't taken too seriously, so long as they can be set aside once the real business of life begins. (But aren't men often blocked in just these same ways?) I had no women models, as we now understand that word—

and that need. I didn't even know many older women who worked. Not only my parents but I myself consciously wanted me to marry and have children. Physical energy was limited. I write slowly. It was the era of *The Feminine Mystique.* And it seems to me even now that the difficulties we all sensed and continue to sense are real and to be respected. I saw clearly how hard it would be for me to make a lasting relationship, bring up children and "live a full life as a woman," while being a committed writer. The women poets I read about were generally not known for their rich, stable sexual and family lives.

Such problems must have faced any young woman of my age who thought of being a poet. Beyond this, each of us can only speak for the problems of her own temperament and her own personal history. As I've already suggested, I was both quite conservative socially at this period and becoming radical in my insights. "Half lover-poet-sybil / Half what the kind nets swallow." An impossible combination. When I first reread the old poems, I was struck by the number that use *seeing* as a metaphor. Seeing equals truth-telling. I wanted to see far, like an astronomer, and I wanted to see through, as if by X-rays. But "The urge to tell the truth / Strips sensuality." Domesticity, too. If the poems have a virtue that makes some of them worth printing even after all these years, despite their immaturities, despite a blocky, half-borrowed rhetorical style, I think it is not only as a historical record but because of their psychological acuteness. At the same time, a woman painter to whom I showed them not long ago commented on how persistently they seek the "bone," how only the very last ("Obligations," "A Bedside Rune") have any concern for human "breathing." There is a kind of corrosive perfectionism running throughout—a perfectionism that made me end "The Door," in its final draft, with a bid for transcendent union, using an image of X-rays for the recognition at zero-level I wanted the lovers to achieve, while another poem about an almost paralyzed affair, "Twins," uses X-rays as an image of destructive knowing.

I can't say I didn't recognize how much, if I gave up poetry, I'd be giving up:

Foresee me now huddled in my kitchen
Like the woman Ronsard wrote to, shelling peas,
Slag-haired, grained like a rock in the Atlantic,
Having survived the age for lovers and
All subsequent ages, married to the bone
In Greenland. . . .

suggests a marriage which, in its dedication to things of the earth and
away from poetry, "will destroy me." "Washing across my face / Look
where they drag and scar—the peas, the children." But the truth is, I
had come to view poetry as even more destructive. I seemed to have
made a mess of my most intimate friendships, and poetry—that gift for
seeing far and seeing through—now looked less like a source of re-
newal (as it had at Oxford) than the house-wrecker. By the winter of
1950–51, though I was still often writing well, I was beginning to be ap-
palled by the images of "guilt, war, disease" that dominated my think-
ing and kept appearing in the poems almost in spite of myself. Poems
like "Meteors" and "After the Bomb Tests" (where Kepler becomes the
"virgin artist" and the atomic-bomb explosion mimics human concep-
tion and birth) were mirrors into which I couldn't bear to gaze for
long.

TEACHING

"I see, you had to survive," said a wise friend recently, rather quickly
laying the old manuscript aside. And indeed, as much as one can by an
act of will, I set about to change my life. In September of 1950 I left
Princeton to go into teaching, something I had believed in humanly
since that summer at Oxford but had kept putting off. I started in at
once at Sarah Lawrence College, which was more, with only a B.A.
and no previous experience, than I deserved. I remember that during
one of my interviews I was asked, "And why do you think you can
teach poetry?" and I answered, "Because it's the one place where I'd as

soon take my own word as anybody else's," though I went on to explain that that didn't mean I thought I was always right! Still, it was eight years before I was given a poetry course. I taught fiction and fiction writing, and to women students. In place of the part-time freelance editing job I was used to, which had left me with free mornings and plenty of free-floating fantasy out of which to write, I was soon working sixty hours a week. I cared very much about those students, and there was everything to learn.

The poems of 1950–51, that first teaching winter, are curiously mixed. I was able to finish several of my angriest Princeton pieces, like "Twins" and "Long View from the Suburbs." I wrote several ambitious new poems ("After the Bomb Tests" started out to be a sonnet-ring) in the old style. At the same time, I was beginning to loosen up, to want to use more natural imagery, but also not to be able to develop all I wrote in the old decisive way. This led to its own kind of despair. I didn't yet want poetry to sound like conversation, but the rhetoric I'd been accustomed to and had tried so hard to perfect ("Head first, face down, into Mercator's world") seemed altogether out of keeping with the life I was now leading. I wrote some rather sweet, static poems about children, landscapes, old men. I don't even remember writing "In a Room with Picassos," where not only the fellow artist but my own role as artist was put to the test. The most satisfying challenge of the year was "Obligations," which later seemed like the last of the old and first of the new—the only poem of the early group to find its way, in somewhat revised form, into my 1969 book. It was the last of the old in that I remember working out the structure quite carefully as a series of abstract geometric figures (the circle that reduces itself to a point, then is opened out again by the "broken shining blade"), which are also of course sexual analogies; but it is also quite an honest poem about an accepted human encounter, with its own built-in griefs, and it is set in a stubble field, by daylight, with real insects humming, rather than against some hallucinated sky or sea. One version makes the sexual tie "our defense, which we shall soon evade"; another, the one I have used here because it seems to be the one I came back to, calls it "our defense, which we cannot evade." It was still a time of uncertainty for me, even crisis.

Otto Rank suggested to Anaïs Nin that women have trouble being artists because they damp down what is destructive in them, therefore they can't create freely either. Nin concludes, "In order to create without destroying, I nearly destroyed myself." By the end of 1951, my awareness of crisis had in fact reached a peak. I who had started out asking for equality with the men I knew now wondered whether I had been "castrating." I had a continual, grinding sense of loss and self-betrayal, which only the daily human wear-and-tear of teaching helped somewhat to offset if not change. It was during this second teaching winter that, almost more than my giving up poems, the poems seemed to give me up. What few I wrote were pale and diffuse, or full of self-pity. When I rewrote, I often blurred earlier insights. I was overworked, my health suffered, above all I wanted to learn how to live. By the time I had gone back to writing and, in 1957, was beginning to publish in magazines, I didn't even want to look back at that first manuscript. I remembered it as more destructive than it could ever possibly have been.

Is this primarily a political story, having to do with how hard it is for a woman to *feel* the freedom that would let her develop as a writer, even when she has it? Is it a tale of personal neurosis? Or is it simply the history of one individual woman, probably more twisted than I've allowed for here by lovers' claims and family ambitions, in which—as in any history—accident too played a part, but whose echoes may reverberate? For we need all the connections we can make.

> *En l'an trentiesme de mon aage*
> Perhaps I shall discover
> That each is coward other
> And drinking shame, creep into time's cage.

ends the birthday poem I wrote at twenty-three, though it was an ending I was never really satisfied with. Maybe, I was saying, instead of feeling "wiser" and more secure by the time I reached thirty, I'd find out instead that to be either "lover-poet-sybil" *or* a housewife would be a kind of cowardice, because I couldn't be both. Since each would be only a half-life, maybe they would add up to the same life? The final "cage" might not be a matter of choice at all but the necessary compromises of aging, of facing myself. Even then I had the foretaste of shame, like a numbing drug.

A Room of My Own, with Windows

I have said that I gave up poetry, but after all it seems as if I never quite gave up the idea of writing. To have been convinced for so long that I gave it up altogether may have been the last deception I practiced on myself in connection with that early work, those early years. For I still have the journal I kept during the winter and spring of 1952–53, the year before I went to the University of Iowa to (as I told everybody) observe teaching methods at the Writers' Workshop there. I hadn't been at Iowa more than three or four weeks before I was deep in stories of my own and, once more, poems. By the second semester the stories had been laid aside. . . . But what the journal documents is that it was started deliberately as a way of getting me back to writing, through the sanity of observed detail, and that I had begun to think seriously about fiction. Fiction might prove a more humane mode than poetry. Did I also have some idea (the journal doesn't say so) that to be a woman short-story writer might be more acceptable than being a woman poet?

Most of all I wanted to get people into what I wrote—people who were not mere projections of my own needs and angers but people walking around and talking, recognizably *other,* as unique and often funny as my students had turned out to be. If seeing was the metaphor for truth-telling in the poems that lay just behind me, seeing from the height of an airplane or with the intensity of X-rays, then looking was what I aimed for by 1953, truly looking at the world around me and trying to record it. I was touched by Ransom's notion that it is the specific detail, intimately rendered, that reveals our love for a subject. Much of the journal is simply notes I took out my New York City windows. In the fall of 1952 I had moved to a walk-up on West Sixteenth Street, between Seventh and Eighth Avenues, and this neighborhood was shocking me awake in a new way. In my mind was that room I always remember, again from the summer of 1947, in heavily shelled St. Mâlo: *Two walls of an old stone building are still standing, up one of which a stone staircase climbs crazily toward nothing. Halfway up, pitched over space and rubble, is cantilevered a brand-new timber box—yellow, fresh-smelling, inhabited—with a potted red geranium in its one immaculate window-square.*

For despite my memory of the strain of those years, the journal is honest, strong, feeling, and it even has a kind of natural gaiety. It speaks of the necessity for changing myself, for finding a new style both of being and writing, to go with the changed realities I now perceived. It explores what might be required for short stories and outlines a good many plots. Because the mechanistic imagery I had used so far had begun to horrify me, and certainly contradicted in intent and almost in coloration what I wanted to do next, it suggests that a new imagery must be found, less like a crustacean's shell. But to change one's images is like trying to revolutionize one's dreams. It can't be done overnight. Nor can it be effected by will. I find one entry reading: "Something seems to have broken in me last year, like a spring breaking.... What broke ... is perhaps the sense that you can build your life by choice. Now I think you build it out of necessities—and that all you can do is answer these necessities in the decentest way possible.... I am trying to learn to lead a decent life and not want to be a great person and, at the same time, know what I have the human right to draw the line at."

"Not want to be a great person." ("To be a man, the crowd's hero.") I was jolted when I discovered those words written out, for how rarely we admit we want to be great persons. Women's need to appear modest, certainly my own need, is almost as powerful as the need to be "nice," and no doubt not at all separate from it.

The journal gives specific reasons for the failure of the poems of the previous five years and even of my whole concept of poetry. Too "musical," for one thing. "I think first of all in terms of a very definite rhythm and structure. Emotionally, too, I think in terms of rhetoric, of an impassioned dramatization of a moment. . . . Now I can no longer capture those moods . . . and so the whole rhetorical machinery seems . . . out of date. My poetry was heroic poetry, and now what I have to say doesn't concern heroes, and I haven't the heart to change the machinery, taking out a screw here and a blade there, to make it something different, and less, than it was. . . . The poetry I have written this year is just empty mechanics or else it hardly comes into being."

Again: "I have a very old-fashioned idea of what poetry should do. It is the soul's history and whatever troubles the soul is fit material for poetry. Therefore I was right to try to write war poems, even if they were often overblown, because no one can live just personally, just observing the workings of his own consciousness, these days. Now I am trying to write [about] love—but giving the quality of the other person."

And finally: "To begin with, love is a joyful recognition of capacities within yourself. It is yourself you fall in love with. Much later, perhaps, the individual with whom you are in love comes to mean more than the condition of 'being in love.' For some people this means a comedown to what they call friendship; for others, it is marriage. . . . The first abstract stage is the stage of poetry. Does the second stage imply fiction, or just a different kind of poetry, a poetry of development rather than passionate lyrical statement?"

How much one would like to be able to argue with one's younger self! And yet was this concept of poetry—that it should be heroic, "musical" (*i.e.,* romantically metrical, with "a very definite rhythm and structure"), and even abstract—so different from that other concept, which I'd been brought up to and wanted to believe, that I should find the *solution* to my life, not just companionship, in a single, other person? (And that I still wanted marriage, the imagery of the last paragraph makes perfectly clear.) The final version of "The Door" showed what a weight this put on the men I knew, as well as on myself. They had to be heroic, and not the least of my mistakes lay in blaming myself when it turned out, humanly enough, to be otherwise.

But most of the journal is not so didactic, nor even particularly meditative. I was living on a half-Irish, half-Puerto Rican block, and I wrote about the boys burning Christmas greens in the gutters in January; about the soft-drink bar where the older boys hung out, smoking, perched on orange crates along the sidewalk, almost under the lee of a crumbling brownstone called "Rainbow"; I recorded the little girls' street games and some of their chants. One day in May an amusement truck came along, shaped like a gigantic popcorn popper with loudspeakers on top, and as the children were jounced down and then up almost to the height of the first-story windows, one cried, "Hey, look at the sky!" From my fire escape I made a rough sketch of the truck body, with approximate dimensions. I thought of the windows across the street from mine as eye-pairs, two to a family, into which I could look and which would sometimes stare back at me out of their separate, never-fully-to-be-understood worlds.

An Art of the Unexpected

My getting back to poems again, the following year, is really another story. I think I am still trying to work out a "poetry of development." And certainly when I first started at Iowa I had to face the embarrassment (to call it by a mild name) of knowing that what I wrote was far weaker, from any standpoint but my own, than what I had been doing three or four years before. It was after all not just a matter of "taking out a screw here and a blade there, to make . . . something different." My whole intention as a writer had changed. In trying for a more generous habit of mind, for instance, whether deliberately or not I set aside the kind of anger that often goes along with sexuality as one of the pivots of my work. I wonder how many women share with me this history, of not having wanted to admit their anger? I did write as an observer, almost too patiently. For a while children, landscapes, old men predominated. It is very difficult to practice any art wholeheartedly and not to compromise, at least now and then, teaching as well as maternal roles, community responsibility. There is the danger of self-centeredness, if not downright selfishness. On the other hand, for writers especially, just because they use words, it is hard to be generous and never to indulge in self-censorship.

These questions that confront women writers (and of course, many men too) are, far more than the questions I opened with, the ones that continue to trouble me. How are we to balance our needs? It's unlikely that any young woman poet today would simply suppress her work, as I did. And I wish I hadn't. Yet I can't be sorry that *The Weather of Six Mornings,* when it finally appeared, was based on certain rather broad human acceptances. I had to get through the perfectionism of those early poems, to learn that no choice is absolute and no structure can save us. If I no longer hesitate to bring out a few pages from that first manuscript, the questions are just as urgent as they ever were. All the more reason, I think, to accept as part of whatever I now am that young, cabined, often arrogant, but questing and vivid self whose banishment I've come to recognize as one more mistaken absolute. For if my poems have always been about survival—and I believe they have been—then survival too keeps revealing itself as an art of the unexpected.

NEW YORK, 1974

3

Dispossessions:

Poems

1968–1973

Messages

1

Ragged and thrashing
the road between me and the ocean—

I trip on stumps.
A gull flies over:

Guilt! guilt! your father is dying!
The woods are studded with poisonous berries.

How smooth they shine
red as tail-lights, inviting—

The roar of a cliff.
From the tip of this plunge of darkness

a few stars telegraph:
Go back. Or else welcome.

2

Approaching my life I am terrified.
Stars in the mud trip me up.

Terrified, I lug stone after stone
up the wide, foot-bruising ladder of night.

Stones in a ring can't define it:
Night.   Lake.   Mirror.   Deep.   Only

Poetry As Continuity

The young doctor dreamed of revolution.
The middleaged revolutionary dreamed of a tree
offering its red berries, thrusting down roots like a woman.

Under miles of snow, under railroad tracks stitched like a suture,
the earth slept all the way to Moscow.
How strangely space is playing the part of time!

What reached the city was only a coincidence
in a life of parades. Zhivago,
you are all we have left, in the end you were scarcely a man.

After the Blackout (1965)

Clocks are wrong, watches
awry; stars still march
slowly across a vault of black glass.

Through a glass I see
how it's all right, cities
burn out their stars but only for a time.

Constellations are curved, pasted
at the rim of the universe.

How it all curves back on us! distance,
a father mourned, estrangement of
east Harlem slums,

night bombing, napalm, the streaming self
in a strait jacket—
We are all contained.

Forgiven. I want to forgive
what was never done to me
outright.

Dream in Which the Routine Quality of My Imagination Is Fully Exposed

Yes they set the house on fire, my father
had an incurable disease, my mother
was ready to die with him, my brother
stood at his desk smiling,
a pacifist.

I knew it would be useless
to try to change their minds, I wrestled
a few keepsakes out of the smoke, I chose
the sofas because
they're so expensive.

Yes I had my grief, I had
to acquire a new life, I thought
now I'll be charged with the murder
of my entire family, who will suppose
only I wanted to survive?

Cemetery in Pernambuco:
Our Lady of Light

(from the Portuguese of João Cabral de Melo Neto)

Nobody lies in this earth
because no river is at rest
in any other river, nor is the sea
a potter's field of rivers.

None of these dead men here
comes dressed in a coffin.
Therefore they are not buried
but spilled out on the ground.

Wrapped in the hammocks they slept in,
naked to sun and rain,
they come bringing their own flies.
The ground fits them like a glove.

Dead, they lived in the open air.
Today they are part of open earth,
so much the earth's that the earth
does not feel their intrusion.

95°

Lost in summer, I worry about your silence.
You stick your head into loneliness as into an oven,
holding out, holding out. . . .
All your friends are out of town.
On the fringe of the park, your building is turning to dust.
Letters come, the phone rings, you sit by your window
balancing yourself like a last glass of water.

While here the boys are diving under the bridges,
a girl is painting a sailboat yellow and green
to the whine of a transistor radio.
I climb to the post office. No mail.
And no need for mail, except the city
lies crouched in its anger behind me, and these unblistered elms
seem hardly real enough yet to write you about.

Holding Out

Letters come, the phone rings, you sit by your window
balancing yourself like a last glass of water.

All over the city the hospitals are crammed with wounded.
Divorce, like marriage, requires two adversaries.

But what is left now is not to exaggerate:
your grief, his grief—these serious possessions.

Dispossessions

1. THINGS

Things have their own lives here. The hall chairs
count me as I climb the steps. The piano
is playing at will from behind three potted plants,
while the photograph of the dead girl in the luminescent hat
glows pink since the lamp lighted itself at four.

We are very humane here. Of course people
go off course sometimes, radio to the outside world
only through typewriter noise or the bathwater running.
And then the empty glasses, the books on health food left around. . . .
But the things have been here longer than we have.

And the trees are older even than furniture.
They were here to witness the original drownings
(because I always think the children drowned, no matter what you
    say).
Last night a voice called me from outside my door.
It was no one's voice, perhaps it came from the umbrella stand.

2. SOUVENIRS

Anyway we are always waking
in bedrooms of the dead, smelling
musk of their winter jackets, tracking
prints of their heels across our blurred carpets.

So why hang onto a particular postcard?
If a child's lock of hair brings back
the look of that child, shall I
nevertheless not let it blow away?

Houses, houses, we lodge in such husks!
inhabit such promises, seeking the unborn
in a worn-out photograph, hoping to break free
even of our violent and faithful lives.

3. INHERITANCES

Malte Laurids, peevish: *And one has*
nothing and nobody, travels about the world
with a few clothes and a satchel of books. What sort of life
is it? without a house, without
inheritances (the Chamberlain's eyeglasses, say,
in a glass case?), *without*
dogs—

Yet he wrote the Chamberlain's death, explaining:
I have taken action against fear, I
have sat all night and written.

And: *Still it is not enough*
to have memories, they
must turn to blood inside you.

A Circle, a Square, a Triangle
and a Ripple of Water

Sex floated like a moon
over the composition. Home
was transpierced, ego
thrust out of line and
shaded. But sex floated
over the unconscious, pulling it
up like a sea in points to
where she dreamed, rolling
on and on, immaculate, a full moon
or a breast full of milk.
Seemingly untouched she
was the stone at the center of
the pool whose circles
shuddered off around her.

Suicide Note

It's not that I'm out of touch—
a child stranded on a shoal
looking back without feeling
at the grownups still playing on the beach.

It's just that everyone else's
needs seem so urgent!
Already I've ceased to exist
at my end of this conversation—

And I wanted to defend you!
The telephone is the invader.
Wreath of electrodes! Love!
No trespassing beyond this point. Anyone found here with dog or
*   gun will be*

A Nightmare of the Suburbs

I'll be in my own room, upstairs,
the door locked, with a gun—
But nobody's coming
yet,

no black bodies
rising like night-flowers from your leafy summer streets,
no axe that splits
the drowsy thighbones of your window frame.

You look in your hand mirror—
They won't get in without a struggle!

But already the meager body
of the pistol begins to wake from his long sleep
of cardboard in the drawer of your bedside table.

Glowing blue-black,
now that he's here
only blood can appease him.

The Earthquake

Two people wakened suddenly by an earthquake
accuse each other: *You pushed me out of bed!*
The floor is cold, they're disgruntled, they start to laugh.
Back to bed. The little hills
just beginning to show dark along the horizon
fold their paws and shove off to sleep again
embracing privacy.

But what can I say for the one who sleeps alone
in a child's cot? *Another dream?*
She imagines she must have parachuted out of bed
to escape.
She accuses herself.
Stubbornly, in a mummy-roll of blankets,
she lies awake explaining her usual day.

Pencil Sketch of Self & Other

When you kissed me it was as if
someone had just stepped lightly out of the room.

How shy I was in any crowd,
and you, how adept!

How I kept you waiting
longer than any boy uncertain of his sex!

Your mother, musical, suicidal,
slept with a thread tied round her nurse's finger

(so I learned a few details), your rich father
photographed beside his swimming pool. . . .

How we almost ruined each other, you
with your hope of children,

I with my body which I took too seriously,
that stunned room. . . .

A story, like *The Garden Party,*
no longer even possible.

Yet I want to forgive us both
as if it still matters.

Waiting

My body knows it will never bear children.
What can I say to my body now,
this used violin?
Every night it cries out strenuously
from its secret cave.

Old body, old friend,
why are you so unforgiving?

Why are you so stiff and resistant
clenched around empty space?
An instrument is not a box.

But suppose you are an empty box?
Suppose you are like that famous wooden music hall in Troy,
    New York,
waiting to be torn down
where the orchestras love to play?

Let compassion breathe in and out of you,
breathe in and out of you

Scaffolding

Poems

1975–1983

(1984)

The Flashboat

1

A high deck. Blue skies overhead. White distance.
The wind on my tongue. A day of days. From the shore a churchbell
    clangs.
Below me the grinding of floes: tiny families huddled together
earth-colored. Let me explain, the ice is cracking free.
They were cut off unawares. From the shore a churchbell clangs.
When the ice breaks up it is spring. No
comfort, no comfort.

2

And here is that part of my dream I would like to forget. The purser
is at his desk, he is leaning toward me out of his seat, he is my torturer
who assumes we think alike. Again and again he questions me as to
which national boundaries I plan to cross. *Are you a political activist?*
No, I'm a teacher. But already the last villagers have been swept out to
sea. We are cruising north of the Arctic Circle. Without haste he locks
my passport away in his breast pocket. Was I wrong to declare myself
innocent?

3

(I did not protest. I spoke nothing but the truth. I never spoke of that
girl who kneeled by her skyscraper window, falling without a sound
through the New York City night.)

4

Now it's our turn. Three A.M.
and the Queen Mary is sinking.
All is bustle—but in grays. Red lanterns crawl here and there.
The crew makes ready the boats. One near me, broad but shallow,
looks safe, women are urged, the captain will be in charge.
Far down now: a trough. A smaller dory rocks
in and out of our lights; black fists grip the oars.
Room only for six—we will
all need to row.
For a moment I hesitate, worrying about my defective blood.
A rope ladder drops over. My voice with its crunch of bone
wakes me: *I choose
the flashboat!*

            work,

                    the starry waters

All These Dreams

All these dreams: the dream of the mountain cabin
where five of us ate off the floor in a bower of pines;
the dream of the house without rooms
where light poured down through the roof on a circular stair
made of glass, and there was one blue rug;
the dream of the workshop where, unmarried and pregnant,
I escaped my grandmother's overfurnished house
for the hollow, cold smell of plaster, warm
smell of sawdust underfoot, shapes
of unfinished objects on clean shelves
as I entered at sunset.

All these dreams, this obsession with bare boards:
scaffolding, with only a few objects
in an ecstasy of space, where through the windows
the scent of pines can blow in, where we eat off the floor
laughing, like Japanese sages—How to begin?
O serenity
that can live without chairs, with only a mat,
maybe a crimson mat, or maybe not even . . .
old smell of clay on a wheel, new smell of boards
just cut, the ring of the sculptor's studio.

Where have I escaped from? What have I escaped to?
Why has my child no father?
I must be halfway up the circular stair.
To shape my own—
                    Friends! I hold out my hands
as all that light pours down, it is pouring down.

Scattered Words for Emily Dickinson

1

Inside the crate, dark
as corn in its sheath   sheet lightning

2

This painting was made in Iowa
under the gold sky of the Great Plains.
In her Puritan white dress
in his fiberboard suit
(the rev. family man, from Philadelphia)
at the conservatory door   they
start forth

flashbulbs!

ochre   orange   flame   black   black   white

Brilliant Pioneer Roots   and
difficult geography the face of a friend:
(brilliant) notes from the painter's (my friend's) catalogue
(difficult) notes from the painter's (a pioneer's) catalogue

3

So the stolid-looking veteran
(G. I. Bill, History of the Language)
told me, speaking of combat:
> *In the least space*
> *between two bodies*
> *there is room*
> *for mystery*

S. Eliason 66: *Double Portrait of Emily Dickinson and the Rev. Charles Wadsworth*

She is just leaving the room.
He fades to a china cup.

Velocity fraught with gold,
with *menace of light,* atomic secrets—
An aroused skin opens over the Great Plains.
October leaves rain down.

Corn in conflagration!
The great retreats of the Civil War!
Marriage in conflagration!

Years—an empty canvas.
She scrawls across radiant space

E . . . I . . . SON! *I made this.* The date.
Name within name.

Evening Star (Georgia O'Keeffe)

Evening Star unfurling like an embryo
all fluid energy
expanding like the galaxy

What happened between your first charged watercolors
leaking blood and fur
and the white lightning of this ideograph?
A message to a friend—
if he saw it he didn't know it was to him

Olympic Rain Forest

I left the shutter open, the camera
flooded with light, the negatives
were abstract and damp as the undersides of leaves.

So much greenish light, I had never
imagined a transfusion of so much tenderness.

Why can't it all be printed? How can I stand here
holding in one hand a fossil fern, in the other
a colored guide from the Sierra Club?

Travel isn't originality. I
left the shutter open.

What I need is a new medium, one that will register
the weight of air on our shoulders, then
how slowly a few hours passed,

one that will show
the print of your heels that morning on the spongy forest floor,
there, not there.

Starting with a Line from Roethke

To have the whole air!
To own, for the moment, nothing.

The purl of a wood-thrush winding down through the blazing
    afternoon.
The least flick of leaves.

Sunlight as energy
but diffused until it becomes the soft clang of poems

approaching from a great way off
out of the cave of the past. . . .

Frida Kahlo's exuberant fruit,
hacked open and sexual, or

cliffs ringing with the calm off Tintagel.
Calm off Tintagel.

The River in All Lights, from
an Upstairs Window

The river in all lights, from an upstairs window:
The river sometimes like a ribbon of blood.
The river with water hyacinths, blood-brown stems
and lilac heads, iron rusting to blue.
The river blue on blue under the sun.
The river nicked with white as the wind rises.
The river darkened to steel, with copper glints,
or elephant-blue under a thunderous sky.
Now the horizon is lost, the opposite shore
lost as the river roils and mirrors itself.
Now there is only a ribbon of glistening mist
we call the river. Now there is only sky.

Jittoku, Buddhist Mystic—15th Century

Everything is blowing, his
skirts are blowing, he stands
hands clasped in enormous sleeves
behind his back, at his feet a
dropped broom. The strokes of the
broom made of dry sticks and the
swoop of a few live pine needles
shiver together, his unruly
chopped-off hair and the fringes
of his girdle all are blowing
eastward. Only the corners of his
mouth defy gravity. He is laughing,
humped against the wind with his bawdy
nostrils wide he is laughing: The
moon! Old boat of the white full moon!

A Mission with the Night

An old black man used to come to our door in Florida during the Depression. He never got lost going home through the dark without a flashlight. He would say, "I got a mission wid' de night."

1

She is like that man
She is like that man carrying his torch of words
She is like the torch of words
She is the poet with her torch of words in exile
She is in exile
She is finding her way
She is finding her way home through a cypress swamp
She is finding her way back on a moonless night
She is like the moon
She is like a ray of the moon or a cypress root
She is like the root uncovering its own source
She is like the ray at an open window
She is an open window
She is not at the source yet
The source is finding her out

2

He came all this way
leaning on his old stick like a flame
a jointed flame, a flame that hums with words

The words soaked up from the earth itself
They reached his fingers, they signified to his heart
They became his eyes that reached into the night

He is at the door
He is standing at the old screen door with his one yellow tooth
smiling, asking for food

Rent

If you want my apartment, sleep in it
but let's have a clear understanding:
the books are still free agents.

If the rocking chair's arms surround you
they can also let you go,
they can shape the air like a body.

I don't want your rent, I want
a radiance of attention
like the candle's flame when we eat,

I mean a kind of awe
attending the spaces between us—
Not a roof but a field of stars.

Conversation by the Body's Light

Out of my poverty
Out of your poverty
Out of your nakedness
Out of my nakedness
Between the swimmer in the water
And the watcher of the skies
Something is altered

Something is offered
Something is breathed
The body's radiance
Like the points of a constellation
Beckons to insight
Here is my poverty:
A body hoarded
Ridiculous in middle age
Unvoiced, unpracticed

And here is your poverty:
A prodigality
That guts its source
The self picked clean
In its shining houses

Out of my nakedness
Out of your nakedness
Between the swimmer in the skies
And the watcher from the water
Something is reached
For a moment, acknowledged
Lost—or is it shelter?
The still not-believed-in
Heartbeat of the glacier

Praise

But I love this poor earth,
because I have not seen another. . . .
                    —OSIP MANDELSTAM

Between five and fifty
most people construct a little lifetime:
they fall in love, make kids, they suffer
and pitch the usual tents of understanding.
But I have built a few unexpected bridges.
Out of inert stone, with its longing to embrace inert stone,
I have sent a few vaults into stainless air.
Is this enough—when I love our poor sister earth?
Sister earth, I kneel and ask pardon.
A clod of turf is no less than inert stone.
Nothing is enough!
In this field set free for our play
who could have foretold
I would live to write at fifty?

The Blue Anchor

The future weighs down on me
just like a wall of light!

All these years
I've lived by necessity.
Now the world shines
like an empty room
clean all the way to the rafters.

The room might be waiting for its first tenants—
a bed, a chair, my old typewriter.

Or it might be Van Gogh's room
at Arles:
so neat, while his eyes grazed among phosphorus.
A blue anchor.

To live in the future
like a survivor!
Not the first step up the beach
but the second
then the third

—never forgetting
the wingprint of the mountain
over the fragile human settlement—

Threads: Rosa Luxemburg from Prison

1. WRONKE, SPRING 1917

You ask what I am reading. Natural science for the most part; I am studying the distribution of plants and animals.

A huge white poplar half fills the prison garden.
All the songbirds love that tree best. The young leaves
sticky all over with a white down
shine in the sun like flowers!
But by now the small birds
(May 23rd) are much too busy to sing.
Hens keep their nests, cocks with their beaks full
streak back and forth. Yesterday—
yes, for the first time in almost three weeks
I caught the *zeezeebey!* of a blue tit
shrilling over the wall.
At fourteen I was proud, I pitied my mother
for telling me Solomon understood the gossip of birds.
Now I'm like Solomon, that quick *zeezeebey!*
roused me to the sorrows of bird life

I must be out of sorts, just now I was reading
how in the name of scientific agriculture
we've drained the swamps, chopped down brushwood and stumps,
cleared away leaves,
while civilized men (according to Professor Sieber)
drove the Redskins from their feeding grounds
in North America

And they made you talk to Karl
through a grating?
I remember in Warsaw
I was on hunger strike, I could barely stand.
My brother came to see me. They propped me in a cage,
a cage within a cage. (I gripped with both hands

to hold myself upright.) From the outer wires
he peered across as at a zoo. *Where are you?* he asked,
again and again brushing away the tears that clouded his glasses

But you make too much of my "equanimity," Sonya.
It is simply my way
when I suffer not to utter a word

Sonyusha, I know I can say this to you, my darling—
You will not promptly accuse me
of treason against socialism. Suppose I am really
not a human being at all but some bird or beast?
I walk up and down my scrap of prison garden—
I'm alone in a field where the grass is humming with bees—
and I feel more at home
than at a party congress. Of course I always
mean to die at my post, in a street fight
or prison. But my first self
belongs to the tomtits more than to our comrades

Still, nature is cruel, not a refuge,
and—you won't mind?—I have to laugh
a little when you ask me, *How can men dare
judge you and Karl?* My little bird,
given the totality of vital forms
through twenty thousand years of civilization,
that's not a reasonable question! Why are there blue tits?
Zeezeebey! but I'm awfully glad there are.
We live in the painfulest moment of evolution,
the very chapter of change, and you have to ask,
What is the meaning of it all? Listen,
one day I found a beetle stunned on its back,
its legs gnawed to stumps by ants; another day
I clambered to free a peacock butterfly

battering half dead inside our bathroom pane.
Locked up myself after six, I lean on the sill.
The sky's like iron, a heavy rain falls, the nightingale
sings in the sycamore as if possessed.
What is the meaning of it all? What is the meaning
of young weeds tufted in the prison wall? young poplar shoots?
underground passages of wasp and wild bee
I try not to shake when I walk? ant highways
straight as the Roman? The wall stones shine with wet,
reddish, bluish—a comfort even on
color-starved winter days—gray and resurgent green

2. Breslau, November–December 1917

I had a vision of all the splendor of war!

Hans is killed
          Now twilight begins at four
N "broke the news"
          Over the great paved courtyard
          hundreds of rooks fly by with a rowing stroke
Such a parade of grief! Why can't friends understand
I need solitude to consider? Why not tell me
quickly, briefly, simply
so as not to cheapen
          Their homecoming caw,
          throaty and muted, is so different from their
          sharp morning caw after food. As if metal balls,
          tossed from one to the other, high in the air,
          tinkled   exchanging the day's news
my last two letters
addressed to a dead man
          stolen greetings
          passed between me and the rooks
          here in the darkening yard
I'm allowed so few letters. But from now on, Sonitchka,
I can talk to you again—I mean on paper—
just as before

If only I could send you
like a starry cloak
the confident joy I feel. I lie awake
in black wrappings of boredom, unfreedom and cold.
A distant train hoots. Now there's the squeak
of damp gravel under the desolate boot
of the midnight guard, who coughs. It becomes a song.

My cell trembles. I'm lying in a field streaked with light.
How can that be? My heart beats. Life itself,
the riddle, becomes the key to the riddle. Even this war,
this huge asylum, this casual misery
in which we drown, this too must be transformed
into something meant, heroic. Like an elemental force,
some flood or hurricane, like an eclipse of the sun,
absurd to judge it! These are the chosen tracks
down which the future must break forth. If only the war lasts. . . .
Meanwhile, I'm deep in geology.
You may find that dry, but it opens up
the vastest conception of nature, the most unified view
of any science. I read
in an intoxication of calm. I look up
to smile at Hans as if he stood in the door.
These forces, these cataclysms that would sweep us away,
we have to accept them
as subjects of study, data for exploration

Eagles, falcons, hawks, owls   All the birds of prey
flying to Egypt   Bird migrations
always a puzzle to me
over the blue Mediterranean
       From Rumania: war trophies
       A hundred head of buffalo
       in Breslau alone
       These beasts, stronger than oxen
       Their horns recurved
       over a skull flat as a sheep's
       Black hide   Huge, soft eyes
Flying with them   so many that the sky floods dark:
nightingales, larks, golden-crested wrens
A cloud of songbirds

Thousands of natural victims
without fear
        Rough army drays
        drawn up in the courtyard where I take my walks
        The load: haversacks, old army tunics, shirts
        darkened, soaked with blood
        Brought here from the front
        for the women prisoners to mend
All of them flying toward a common goal:
to drop half dead
beside the Nile
and sort themselves into territories and species
        Today a towering dray
        dragged by a team of freshly broken beasts
        The soldier-driver
        beating and beating with the butt of his whip
        Even our woman gatekeeper protesting
        One ripped and bleeding
        its stiff hide torn
        the look on its black face like a weeping child's
        The rest of the team
        half dead   standing while the dray was emptied at last
        perfectly still
Reading
how on the long flight south larger birds
often carry the small   Reading:
cranes
sighted in amazing numbers along the coast
with a twittering freight
of songbirds on their backs
        Eyes
        of the bleeding   My own dark
        handsomely photographed eyes

Tears / negative
Tears / negative
Tears / negative   of my own face dead
skull beaten in and
drowned
The suffering of a dearly loved brother could hardly have affected me more
profoundly
As if all the birds declared
        Brother! I am one with your
a "truce of God!"
        one with your pain, your helplessness, your longing
        one with you in my helplessness

        The music of the songbirds
        in the flowery meadows of Rumania
        The mythical herdsman's call

Meanwhile the women prisoners were jostling one another as they busily
unloaded the dray and carried the heavy sacks into the administration build-
ing. The driver, hands in his pockets, was striding up and down the court-
yard smiling to himself as he whistled a popular air. I had a vision of all the
splendor of war!

3. BRESLAU, SPRING 1918

*I am so looking forward to spring. It is the only thing one
never gets tired of.*

My window looks on the red brick wall
of the men's prison
        My petition for release
        has been rejected
Just the crests of trees
blur above the roofs of the lunatic asylum
        My petition   even for a brief furlough
        rejected
Here, unfortunately, that is all one can see
over the high brick wall
        It seems I am going to stay here
        till we have conquered the whole world

This lovely world! If only we could walk through it, talk
freely together, weep over it. Sonyusha,
whenever I don't hear from you, I fear you're driven,
whipped by the winds of your loneliness,
helpless as a young leaf. The days grow long,
the clouds rush by. Our chalky soil,
which doesn't yet show it's been planted,
streams with changing lights. Get out as much as you can.
Darling, the earth is faithful, the one thing
fresh but yet faithful. Be my eyes for me,
let me see all you see

This March seems fateful. Strange, to hear them singing
far off from the grounds of the lunatic asylum:
nightingales, wrynecks, golden orioles
(that "Whitsun bird"), never heard till April here,
never heard till May   laughing and

fluting in the
pale gray light
before dawn
What is the reason for this premature migration?
Is it meant for Berlin too?
Sonya, for my sake
please go to the Botanical Gardens,
let me hear all you hear,
for over and above the outcome of the Battle of Cambrai,
this really seems to me
the most important issue of the day

May 12th. Fragments of the established world
flame and submerge, they tear away. Day by day
we witness fresh catastrophes   Strange
how most people see nothing, most people
feel the earth firm under their feet when it is
flaming
*whereas my concern for organic nature is by now almost morbid in its
intensity*
Dusk: down below in the court
a young crested lark is running with short steps,
fluttering up and piping. I listen for the soft *hweet! hweet!*
of the parent birds seeking food. It makes me ill
to see such suffering
             I feel how you   must be suffering
and I can do nothing to help
My buffaloes still come, my foolish starling
is missing
             suffering because you can't "live"
sparrows and pigeons
follow me about like dogs
for a crumb

It's no use telling myself I am not responsible for all the hungry little larks
in the world. Logic does not help
>Never mind, we shall live   shall live
>through grand events
>Have patience

Thus passing out of my cell in all directions
are fine threads connecting me
with thousands of birds and beasts
>You too, Sonitchka, are one of this urgent company
>to which my whole self throbs, responsive

Write soon. Please tell me how Karl is.
Perhaps Pfemfert can find you *The Flax Field*
by Streuvels. For these Flemish authors
not Flanders alone has become the beloved
but all nature   beyond even
the radiant skin
of the globe

Green Notebook, Winter Road

Poems

1981–1993

(1994)

I

On the

Edge of the

Moment

The Green Notebook

There are 64 panes in each window of the Harrisville church
where we sit listening to a late Haydn quartet. Near the ceiling clouds
build up, slowly brightening, then disperse, till the evening sky
glistens like the pink inside of a shell over uncropped grass,
over a few slant graves.

At Sargent Pond the hollows are the color of strong tea.
Looking down you can see decomposed weeds and the muscular bronze
    and green
stems of some water lilies. Out there on the float
three figures hang between water and air, the heat breathes them, they no
    longer speak.
It is a seamless July afternoon.

Nameless. Slowly gathering. . . . It seems I am on the edge
of discovering the green notebook containing all the poems of my life,
I mean the ones I never wrote. The meadow turns intensely green.
The notebook is under my fingers. I read. My companions read.
Now thunder joins in, scurry of leaves. . . .

Ordinary Detail

I'm trying to write a poem that will alert me to my real life,
a poem written in the natural speech of the breakfast table,
of a girl spooning yogurt, pausing, the spoon held aloft
while she gestures toward the exact next turning of her thought.

It would have to be a poem dense with ordinary detail
the way the sun, spilling across walnut and balled-up napkins,
can pick out cups, plates, the letter from which someone has just read
    aloud,
with evenhanded curiosity, leaving behind a gloss of pleasure.

And yet this poem too must allow for the unseen.
Last night the girl dreamed of a triple-locked door
at the head of a short flight of steps. Why couldn't she get in?
How to take possession of that room? Will it be hers to keep?

Remembering, she loses track of her sentence, frowns suddenly, smiles,
excusing herself to the others. A friend's brother died of AIDS.
Sensuality is not the secret; it's more like redemption, or violence. . . .
The girl is walking furiously, under a mild, polluted sky.

My friend

Sylvia said: *When I was younger—*
you know how in the work of most composers
a single line dominates, the melody line?—
Well, years ago I'd think only about my daughter
or only about my marriage, about how to sing,
what Freud meant or some friend. . . . But in Bach,
every voice is equal, each line has invention.
That's how it is for me now, life and death are equal,
I'm neither going up the hill nor down. . . .
                            She paused, then extended her fingers
like Landowska addressing the keyboard. *But I don't know,* she broke off,
whether I'm making myself clear. . . .

My Mother in Three Acts

At the top of the hill you were Muriel,
pale but still powerful as a Sumo wrestler,
generous, mother of mysteries held in reserve.
You were already dead then; I knew I couldn't save you.
In the nursery school room I began to rearrange
brightly colored clay figures: *la Sagrada Familia.*

Tripping down the hill you were Betty,
blond and still fashionable but too thin,
needling me, cosseting me. Dying of cancer
only sharpened your wit. I knew I couldn't save you—
I could barely even keep up! Mother of the quick retort,
of the enchanting story, mother of gifts and dissatisfactions.

At the bottom of the hill just as we reached the
house I had rented, I glimpsed a fugitive girl,
face turned aside toward the woods, slipping away
in a seagreen Japanese kimono; her hair was brown.
Was it you, mother of boyishness, mother of
deception, who saved me once, the one who evades me still?

What the Seer Said

She said I would see the future,
that is to say, my father,
through an ophthalmologic device.

That man was no good, she warned,
but I persisted: *No one,
no one has done me any harm.*

The machine moved on silent wheels.
She fastened my eyes to two wells.
I was pasted to the deep.

The first image was of jangling
kaleidoscopic angles;
the second, inchoate dark.

From a constricted throat
I brought a few words: *My father
was a generous man—but remote.*

At *remote* the darkness unveiled
a mist-becalmed lake and pale
sky and hills like loaves—

blue on blue on blue,
undramatic, unconfused
as the fan of Ma-Yuän—

So this was my father's house!
this courteous, ancestral place!
I lifted my eyes, in relief,

and tasted the mortal cold.
I sat down by the water's edge, old,
deprived, at home, at peace.

Estrangement

You dream someone is leaving you, though he says kindly, *It's not that*
   you're cold
or *After all you're an affectionate person.*

You can't explain how hard it is to explain or even to write this poem
so you blurt, *I was ashamed, they put me in the class for remedial speech.*

The doctor leans forward: *Do you feel you have failed me recently?*
The dream answers through you: *I am locked in a struggle with the truth.*

(I was ashamed, I couldn't speak, they voted me out of the shelter.
Like Rousseau's Sleeping Gypsy I lay exposed to the nuclear night
till a dog found my throat.)

You watch your own back growing smaller up the beach.

Long, Disconsolate Lines

in memory of Shirley Eliason Haupt

Because it is a gray day but not snowy, because traffic grinds by outside,
because I woke myself crying *help!* to no other in my bed and no god,
because I am in confusion about god,
because the tree out there with its gray, bare limbs is shaped like a lyre,
but it is only January, nothing plays it, no lacerating March sleet,
no thrum of returning rain,
because its arms are empty of buds or even of protective snow,
I am in confusion, words harbor in my throat, I hear not one confident tune,
and however long I draw out this sentence
it will not arrive at any truth.

It's true my friend died in September and I have not yet begun to mourn.
Overnight, without warning, the good adversary knocked at her door,
the one she so often portrayed
as a cloud-filled drop out the cave's mouth, crumpled dark of an old garden
    chair. . . .
But a lyre-shaped tree? yes, a lyre-shaped tree. It's true that at twenty-four
in the dripping, raw Iowa woods
she sketched just such a tree, and I saw it, fell in love with its half-heard lament
as if my friend, in her pristine skin, already thrashed by the storm-blows ahead,
had folded herself around them,
as if she gave up nothing, as if she sang.

Mourning Picture

"For John Berryman (1914–1972)" by Shirley Eliason (1929 1988)

A shower of stones. Volcano? *There is no color.*
As if he would never stop falling. Unwritten stones.
The unwritten storm around me. Ashes. Black earth.
Searing, dissolving. . . .
                        When I heard of your death
I thought you could never stop painting, I thought
Even the rocks grow pregnant. Frog spawn. Scum.
The beach is quilted with stones about to hatch.
See, they are crawling inland. *Messengers of chance—*
each stone still glistening from its watery birth. . . .
Your going was private, natural. *Not to be lost:*
two hands fallen open, splayed and very small,
and the abrupt head, indecipherable still.

For the Recorder of Suicides

With a pocketful of stones
one walked toward the water,
propped her head in the oven,
broke his body on the beach.

And did they *discern*
something important
before the soft impact of
nothing at all?

Your words, Shirley,
who just as succinctly
left us in September
for a reserve unsought,

left me here doodling
on a secondhand typewriter.
Composure wears the heart out. Child—
where he stopped the car, the stones.

Nothing I Meant To Keep

Nick said, radiant, being helped upstairs
by a girl, *What's more*
I could marry you in an hour!
That woke me up! but could I marry him?
No, no, my heart cried, from its demure shell.
The girl I was at twenty-three,
that shackled-with-politeness girl,
shook her head, but look, she has turned gray,
arms still locked across my breast.
Breast: ash and translucence now.
Heart: old spark, nothing I meant to keep—
Conversations, or nothing.

Bloodroot

Reading your words
to find they are
just your words. . . .

Waking:
what is this heaviness? only
a matter of money, or closure. Oh yes, the lease,
the rent is going up.

During the war
how I shouted at my mother:
It's only a thing! A thing got broken, suppose
some friend had been killed!

Reading your words.
Remembering how we were friends
in, say, 1974.

Fifteen years ago now, and the whole body
changes, every living cell,
in seven years, and seven years,

and now this one:
fragile as bloodroot,

releasing its unhurried freshness,
half earth, half air.

The Calling

All the voices of the sea called *Muriel!*
Muriel from the Irish *Muirgheal,* meaning
muir, sea, plus *gel,* bright, or in Old English
pure, clean, from the Greek for eyeball

> You who equated *women, ships, lost voices,*
> who lost your speech, then your clear vision,
> who loved flying, sailing, drove a fast car
> with the calm of a centaur, lost your gangrenous toe

from *mori,* body of water, root of Old English *mere,*
a pond or possibly mermaid

> You whose erect carriage was like a figurehead's,
> who lay down outside the Senate, stood by the Korean jail,
> dropped once at a reading of Smart's "Rejoice in the Lamb"
> like a tree felled in the church

whence our cognates *cormorant,*
ultramarine

> Now I perceive what the calling is
> here by this estuary,
> I a year younger than you were when you died
>
> Body of brightness! I trace your undulant tones
> tossed on a clearing wind
>
> whose last, next book was to be FINDINGS
> whose magnified eye stares out past Hariot's trail,
> who crossed out *to,* wrote *from*

I a lost voice
moving, calling you
on the edge of the moment that is now the center.
To   From the open sea

2

Family

Stories

Hotel de Dream

Justice-keepers! justice-keepers!
for Muriel Rukeyser and James Wright

Suppose we could telephone the dead.
Muriel, I'd say, can you hear me?
Jim, can you talk again?

And I'd begin to tell them the stories they loved to hear:
how my father, as a young boy, watched Cora Crane
parade through the streets of Jacksonville with her girls
in an open barouche with silver fittings;
how the bay haunches gleamed as they twitched off flies,
polished hooves fetched down smartly into the dust,
ostrich feathers tickled the palates of passers-by.

Muriel, I'd say, shall we swing along Hudson Street
underneath the highway and walk out together on the docks?

. . . the river would be glittering, my grandmother
would be bargaining
with a black man on a dock in Jacksonville;
grapefruit and oranges would be piled up like cannonballs
at the fort in Old St. Augustine . . .

I'll never put you in a nursing home, you said early that year,
I promise, Jane, I'll never put you in a nursing home.

Later Cora Crane showed her dogs right next to my aunt's.
They had a good conversation about bloodlines
amidst the clean smells of kennel shavings and well-brushed dog
but never, of course, met socially
although she had dined with Henry James.

Jim, I'd say, remember that old poem "The Faithful"
you helped me by caring for? how what we owe to the dead
is to go on living? More than ever
I want to go on living.

But now you have become part of it, friends of my choosing years,
friends whose magnificent voices
will reverberate always, if only through machines,
tell me how to redress the past,
how to relish yet redress
my sensuous, precious, upper-class,
unjust white child's past.

Mary Coldwell

How short their lives were then, but how crammed!
She must have been seventeen when she finished normal school
in Tennessee and began to teach math
to boys taller than she was. No picture of her survives,
but I see her on horseback like my high-spirited aunt:
there's a skin of ice in the ruts of the schoolhouse road. . . .

A scene out of Cather or Laura Ingalls Wilder,
purely American, almost hardscrabble South
or pioneer Gothic. And yet I could have known her.
What ardor in their mother caused my uncle to dream
King Kong slavering at the window, while my father would explain
I like to think of my mind as a machine?

From the Journal Concerning My Father

I

It all started with the maps. Hanging in the living room, the hall, on the way up the stairs, were the old maps of Florida, the flowery land. One showed an Indian woman carrying her child, one showed beavers building a dam and all the plantation sites around Charleston, one showed the round world colored yellow and blue and had been drawn only three years after the great voyage of Magellan. One dull black and white map, a government document, showed Fort Cooper, an outpost in the Seminole Wars.

And then there were the family stories. My father's grandfather, that fierce and unrelenting man, told my father about sailing around Cape Horn in a clipper ship, on his way to the Gold Rush, and how he had come back penniless on the back of a burro right across the Isthmus of Panamá. Even before that his mother had sent him to Spain to trace the genealogy of her family in the Royal Libraries of Seville. My father's grandfather maintained that the true history of Florida would never be written till the royal archives could be opened and transcribed.

He disowned his first-born son—one of two who survived to manhood—for doing the honorable thing and marrying a Minorcan fisherman's daughter, from St. Augustine. The Spaniards had looked down on the Minorcans, because some had the blood of slaves. Great-Uncle Charlie was in Congress, till he broke with his party over Free Silver.

Even in my father's boyhood they still kept Spanish hours in Florida. His grandfather unlocked the doors to his law office at seven every morning, came home for the big dinner of the day at one, took his siesta, then returned to the office from four or five until eight. At nine he presided over (but did not share in) a cold supper. Often the whole family would sit out on the porch afterwards with newspapers wrapped around their ankles to keep off the mosquitoes, enjoying the cool of the evening. Probably he wore a white linen suit, and on the way to the office a fine Panamá hat, and smoked Havana cigars. His sons would take off their hats to him in the street and bow but, preoccupied, he would not recognize them.

My young father slept with a loaded pistol under his pillow every night, such was the incidence of crime in Jacksonville.

Uncle Merian believed America had never paid back her debt to Kosciusko. After the War To End Wars, he flew for Poland, strafing from his single-engine plane the toy bands of Russian cavalry. Then he was in Russian prison camp, starving for bread and books. Later he dined with Haile Selassie, in Abyssinia, whose warriors still wore chain mail. In Persia he crossed mountains higher than the Alps on foot, with the Bakhtiari, to find grass for their flocks. His was the first team to film an elephant stampede from underneath. With all his heart he believed that film would revolutionize the study of anthropology. At home we read about his exploits in *Asia* magazine or *The National Geographic*—back copies kept in the chest at the turn of the stairs in my grandmother's tall, quiet house—or pored over occasional postcards. One postcard showed him squinting into the sun from under his pale topi hat, the white gibbon ape on his shoulder.

He had not yet dreamed of King Kong.

At home, my father seemed the steady older brother, genius of music and gardens. As a boy he had built a boat on my grandmother's veranda and launched it one day with his best friend on the St. John's River, just down the end of the block. Taking along my ten-year-old aunt as crew, they set sail down the Inland Waterway for a weeklong trip. As a lawyer he drove constantly up and down the state in his old Model A. But on Sundays he dug in the flowerbeds; restlessly, he moved the japonica bush, which consequently never bloomed. I would stand beside him sometimes, gazing out at the river, smelling the good smell of turned earth. Below the bluff he kept chickens, ducks, guinea fowl. He loved exotic birds and showed them at the Florida state fair. He was a ham radio operator, and we listened to Lily Pons, with her high, thread-like voice, all the way from New York, by some miracle of the short wave.

It was he who collected the maps.

2

Live oak or magnolia, I rarely looked up at the leaves but only felt their cave-like shade and something like rope burn on the insides of my thighs. Gazing out at water or air, often I would sit astride. Below me the exposed root plunged over the bluff toward the river and halfway down buried itself again in earth. On the last day we lived in that place, I slipped away to say goodbye to the tree. I lay along the root full length and tried to breathe into my own body its peaceful, tidal pulse. From a great way off I heard a trunk lid slam, my mother's voice. . . .

Goodbye! Goodbye to the river, to the sentinel tree that seemed to measure the depth of the sky! A procession of ants of the same rusty black or eggplant color began to circumnavigate the bark just below my wrist. Goodbye to the umbilical root that for nine years had fastened me to this earth!

> *the earth that is nowhere*
> *that is the true home*

3

Earth-spirit, wood-spirit, stone,
father, Other, exposed root

I said goodbye to by the river, where
are you now? I fondle a glass eye.

The eye reflects leaves, stars,
galaxies. . . . Space
was always my demon, the unreachable.
From a black hole, a wavering
flute song, readable.

4

In 1935 he told his new friend, the professor of music—gazing short-sightedly out across his new flowerbeds—that soon there would be regular commercial air travel to Europe and the Orient.

He flew all over Ireland with Lindbergh, in a two-seater plane, to pick out the very best site—at Foynes, near the mouth of the Shannon—for the new airport.

He was delighted to discover, on President DeValera's desk, when he called to negotiate landing rights, a volume of poems by Father Flynn, his grandmother's favorite, who had been the Sweet Singer of the Confederacy.

In 1940 he explained to my brother that the United States had never engaged in a war in which someone bearing the family name had not taken part.

He saw in Vietnam the beginning of a long imperial decline.

When in 1965 I asked him to write something about his family for the grandchildren, he replied: "When I was a boy in the South, after Reconstruction, you had to choose whether to spend your life going forward or looking back. I have never looked back."

My father said Law should precede Man into Space.

He said the circumference of the earth was too small for intelligent aircraft design or navigation.

In 1951, before Sputnik, he said we must decide the legal limits of the upper air. At what point does the atmosphere grow so thin that the concept of national sovereignty becomes meaningless?

Did he die still hoping that human justice could precede technology into the uncharted silences that had terrified Pascal?

Childhood in Jacksonville, Florida

What is happening to me now that loved faces
are beginning to float free of their names
like a tide of balloons, while a dark street
wide enough only for carriages, in a familiar city,
loses itself
to become South America?

Oh I am the last member of the nineteenth century!
And my excitement about sex, which was not of today,
is diffusing itself in generosity of mind.

For my mind is relaxing its grip, and a fume
of antique telephones, keys, fountain pens, torn roadmaps,
old stories of the way Nan Powell died
(poor girl!) rises in the air
detached but accurate—
almost as accurate
as if I'd invented them.

Welcome then, poverty!
flights of strings above the orange trees!

The Hobby Lobby

A stalwart country woman
in a clean, flowered smock, she explained
how she would get up before sunrise

in Tennessee to gather
cobwebs at first light.
How, as if layering a poultice,

she mashed them together, still dewy;
they made a sort of rug,
gray, slightly elastic.

Cobwebs are famous healers
if you mash them into a cut
but hers became spongy beds

for 2-inch-square watercolors
done with the tiniest brush.
The crowd seemed alert, not bored.

The paintings were certainly novel!
mountains, sunsets, cows
in colors coagulated—

My mother gave an odd shudder.
Imagine July, then August,
in Flushing Meadows, *talking*.

My father's second cousin
(once removed) went on with her spiel.
She didn't recognize us

or did she? Mother worried
all the way home on the train.
My father might not *say,*

but they had more in common than blood:
she had made it to the Hobby Lobby
of the 1939 World's Fair.

Class

How the shrimp fisherman's daughter did a handstand against the
schoolyard fence
proving she owned no drawers
just as my grandmother's old black Packard drove up like a hearse

How we dug in the woods for pirate gold
and found only the bootleggers' empties

Wanda's Blues

Ortega Public School, 1932

Wanda's daddy was a railroadman, she was his little wife.
Ernest's sister had a baby, she was nobody's wife.
Wanda was the name and wandering, wandering was their way of life.

Ernest's sister was thirteen, too old for school anyway.
When Ernest couldn't pass third grade, they kept him there anyway,
hunched up tight in a littler kid's desk with his hair sticking out like hay.

But Wanda was small and clean as a cat, she gave nothing away.

At school the plate lunch cost ten cents, milk was a nickel more.
Shrimps were selling for a nickel a pound—those shrimpers' kids were real
    poor,
they lived in an abandoned army camp, the bus dropped them off at the door.

Gossip in the schoolyard had it that Wanda swept and sewed
and cooked the supper for her daddy when he wasn't on the road.
She never told where she ate or she slept, how she did her lessons, if she had an
    ol' lamp. . . .
That wasn't the traveling man's code.

Wanda was smart and watchful, we let her into our games.
Wanda always caught on quick whether it was long division or games.
She never gave a thing away except for her lingering name.

I would say it over: *Wanda   Wanda*

April, and school closed early. We never saw her again.
Her daddy loved an empty freight, he must have lit out again.
Wanda-a-a-a the steam whistle hollered. O my American refrain!

The Past

It seemed, when I was a child, as if you could just reach back and rummage in the 19th century. For instance the ear doctor took me on his knee and later my mother said, *His uncle fought in the War of 1812.* How could that be? It was 1929. And his father had been a famous general for the Confederacy. Then there was Cousin Josiah, U. S. Congress, Retired. He told my mother never to trust anyone who said he had grown up before stoves unless he could tell you how to turn a flapjack. The correct way (in Cousin Josiah's house they were still cooking at the great open fireplace until he was 17) is to pour the batter out along the scorching hearth, wait till the edges begin to curl, slide a greased string underneath, and Flip! Cousin Josiah also told of two ancient people of color who had been born on the family place—once a plantation—in Delaware. *All they knew* was (in the old man's case) how to plant and ret and comb flax, and (in the old woman's) how to spin it. Every year she wove not much more than a single linen handkerchief. They had never been man and wife, nor were they sister and brother, but Cousin Josiah hoped they could die in the same winter, as they had lived. His son was a Quaker witness, whose safe conduct from the Gestapo meant he could enter any prison in Paris during the Nazi Occupation.

How have we come so far? How did we live through (in the persons, for me, of my father, of my uncle) radio, aviation, film, the conquest through exploration of Equatorial Africa, Persia, and Siam? My father thought the moon-walk silly, there were more promising worlds.

And how do I connect in my own body—that is, through touch—the War of 1812 with the smart rocket nosing its way via CNN down a Baghdad street? How much can two arms hold? How soon will my body, which already spans a couple of centuries, become almost transparent and begin to shiver apart?

Being Southern

1

It's like being German.
Either you remember that yours was the defeated country
(*The South breeds the finest soldiers,* my uncle said,
himself a general in one of his incarnations)
or you acknowledge the guilt, not even your own guilt, but

Can any white person write this, whose ancestors once kept slaves?

2

Of course there were "good" Germans.

My father was still under 30, a passionate Wilsonian, when he was
named a delegate to the 1916 Democratic Convention. By the end of
the first evening he had discovered that eleven of the other Florida
delegates were members of the Klan, he couldn't answer for the
twelfth, he was number 13.

Only a few years later he argued for, and won, token black represen-
tation on the Jacksonville school board.

And my aunt as a girl went into the sweatshops to interview Cuban
cigar workers, all women. She founded the first Girl Scout troop in the
South for, as she put it, *colored children.* True, it was segregated. But it
was the first.

Take your guilt to school. Read your guilt in your diplomas or the
lines of the marriage ceremony. Face your guilt head-on in the eyes of
lover, neighbor, child. Ask to be buried in your guilt.

Of course they were paternalistic. I honor their accomplishments.
What more have I ever done?

When is memory transforming? when, a form of real estate?

3

Transplanted "north" in 1934 I never questioned
a town that received its distinguished refugees
with a mix of pride and condescension: the specialist in Christian
    iconography
in her man-tailored suits, Einstein *like a disembodied spirit*
pacing our leafy sidewalks. Only because my best friend lived next
    door
would I glimpse him, sometimes at twilight, tuning his violin
as his back yard filled up with tents

But why can't I remember the actual men and women who slept in
those tents, among patches of ragged tigerlilies? the children with
skinny arms, who would soon be passed along . . . ?

All he could vouch for. Not famous. At their backs
the six million.

Seventeen Questions About King Kong

*The most amazing thing I know about Jane Cooper
is that she's the niece of King Kong.*

—James Wright

Is it a myth? And if so, what does it tell us about ourselves?

Is Kong a giant ape, or is he an African, beating his chest like a responsive gong?

Fay Wray lies in the hand of Kong as in the hand of God the Destroyer. She gives the famous scream. Is the final conflict (as Merian C. Cooper maintained) really between man and the forces of nature, or is it a struggle for the soul and body of the white woman?

Who was more afraid of the dark, Uncle Merian or his older sister? She was always ready to venture downstairs whenever he heard a burglar.

When he was six his Confederate uncle gave him Explorations and Adventures in Equatorial Africa by Paul du Chaillu, 1861. Does that island of prehistoric life forms still rise somewhere off the coast of the Dark Continent, or is it lost in preconscious memory?

Is fear of the dark the same as fear of sexuality? Mary Coldwell his mother would have destroyed herself had she not been bound by a thread to the wrist of her wakeful nurse. What nights theirs must have been!

Why was I too first called after Mary (or Merian) Coldwell, till my mother, on the morning of the christening, decided it was a hard-luck name?

How does our rising terror at so much violence, as Kong drops the sailors one by one into the void or rips them with his fangs, resolve itself into shame at Kong's betrayal?

Is Kong's violence finally justified, because he was in chains?

Is King Kong our Christ?

Watch him overturn the el-train, rampage through the streets! But why is New York, the technological marvel, so distrusted, when technologically the film was unsurpassed for its time?

Must the anthropologist always dream animal dreams? Must we?

Kong clings to the thread of the Empire State Building. He wavers. Why did Uncle Merian and his partner Schoedsack choose to play the airmen who over and over exult to shoot Kong down?

He said: *Why did I ever leave Africa?*—and then as if someone had just passed a washcloth over his face: *But I've had a very good marriage.*

Clementene

I

I always thought she was white, I thought she was an Indian
because of her high-bridged nose, coin-perfect profile
where she sat in an upstairs window, turning sheets sides-to-the-middle—
There are so many things wrong with this story,
Muriel, *I could not tell you*—

Her cheeks were oddly freckled, and her hair would be squeezed down
into a compact, small knot at the nape, gray as chicken wire, gray
as the light, unaffectionate glance her eyes would give
if she lifted them from her work.
No child would interrupt her.

She came twice a year to do the sewing, she slept in the house,
but her meals were brought up, so that she dined by the Singer,
now and then staring fixedly across the river. She joined neither white
in the dining room nor colored in the kitchen.
Her wishes were respected.

Later I saw the same light, disconcerting gaze and futuristic planes
in Oppenheimer's face, but she looked most like my grandmother's friend
    Miss Gertrude
who taught me to tat. Once we moved north, Mother confided
of the *two finest families* in Jacksonville, no one could be sure
whose father was her father.

2

Muriel, I never told you, I never revealed how Clementene
died in our house a white woman and was claimed by her black
    daughter.

How she *flung up her arms* in wild grief
so different from Clementene's reserve.

How she *hollered and called on Christ Jesus,*
flinging her body from side to side at the foot of the staircase.

How the police arrived, it was nine o'clock at night,
long past my bedtime.

How I leaned over the stair rail,
unnoticed for once, as their torches burst in.

It seemed as if tumultuous shadows
crawled through the door, odors of pinestraw, magnolia, river
    bottom—

They are carrying a blanketed stretcher.
Now the daughter follows, still whimpering into my mother's small-
    boned shoulder.

I had seen how a mother could be mourned.
Now I watch my mother shiver and pull away.

Why, if I was not an accomplice,
did I feel—do I feel still—this complex shame?

How Can I Speak for Her?

First there is my little grandfather, I think he is no more than four or five. Anyway it must be after the War, and after his twin brother, his only sister, and his mother have all perished in one of the yellow fever epidemics that swept the low countries of Georgia and South Carolina in the wake of Sherman's march. He is living with his grandmother, the "Castilian." And where is his stiff-necked father, lately of the Confederate Treasury, who once rounded Cape Horn in a clipper ship and returned from California on muleback, right across the Isthmus of Panamá, but was deemed too frail to bear arms? Once, famously, he had nursed the sick and dying in Savannah, but his own young wife he could not save. Once already, through overstrain, he had entirely lost his speech. Is he still head of the Southern Masonic Female College, or ("his health failing") has he departed for Florida, where (but it is Reconstruction?) he will serve in the first postwar legislature of that violent and rudimentary state?

I believe it is Athens, Georgia, I believe it must be Jacksonville; either way I imagine an ill-painted house on a swept street somewhere near the outskirts of town. But of course I don't know where they lived really, I only know my grandfather is playing on the porch at his grandmother's feet. Maybe she is in a rocking chair, mending. In front of them stretches the dusty street, parched white by the sun, empty even of animals. I would like to imagine a sleeping dog, whose neck skin twitches as he dreams, or a chicken or two pecking in the dirt—but probably there are no chickens left, in this summer when so much has already been eaten or long since carried away.

What follows now is confused—but after all there is no film-maker here, to concentrate the image not only in space and light but also in time, and speculation. Down the street limps an old black woman, a woman nobody knows (in this town where everybody, black or white, is acquainted with everyone else). I think she must be complaining a bit, or singing, just under her breath. Has she finally limped away from some burned plantation where she was a slave for forty-odd years, having refused to leave earlier? And if so, where does she live now? Never mind, she has certainly not passed this way before, along this particular road, at just this hour when my great-great-grandmother chances to look up from her shaded and peeling porch. But she must live somewhere nearby, for from this day forward she will come every week, limping through sun and rain, till one of the two old women dies.

So what does my little grandfather see, as he too lifts his eyes from his imaginary wars, where with unfailing regularity the twigs called Yankees are beaten back by the brave twigs called Confederates? Perhaps it is no surprise to him that the stranger is of a peculiarly deep, unmixed black color, that her face is shining but scarred, that she wears a clean headrag with ample, nodding wings above her bleached-out, worn slave dress. Later, certain white people would say the "best" slaves came from the Guinea Coast, and my grandfather would say that if the South had just been let alone, of course the slaves would soon have been freed, slavery being un-Christian and also against the natural law. But at four or five, I think he hardly scans the new arrival. Had she been a chicken, he would have noticed her.

His grandmother starts up from her chair—now *that* is a surprise, this woman whose severity and composure are almost never shaken, who cradles the newborn and the dying with even-handed skill. Who lost her own mother at eight, her father at fourteen, who was immediately married off for propriety's sake, who followed her North American husband from the home plantation in Cuba to the rougher hills of Georgia, who with her surviving children followed him again to flat, malarial north Florida (always the destination must have seemed wilder, more poverty-stricken and remote), only to refugee back, a widow, right into the path of Sherman's troops. Who years ago had sent her eldest son, the frail one, to find out the history of her family in the Royal Libraries of Seville. Who called herself Castilian, though she was almost certainly half French, and would live to scold my little grandfather for the miserable accent with which he spoke any foreign language they attempted to teach him at school. . . . Am I doing her justice, I wonder? this exile who, often hungry herself now, must provide not only food but the will to live for her son's defenseless sons? How much is fact, how much fond family embroidery? The one thing that is clear, that has come down without question through five generations—splendid or chilling, depending on the tale-teller, incomprehensible or simply necessary, depending on your receipt for survival—is her pride.

Slave-mistress from childhood, when the women ran the plantations. Familiar, since childhood, with the lost markings of at least two tribes. . . .

What my grandfather remembered, all those many years later, was that she called out in a language none of them knew she knew, a language no one had heard her speak before, from so deep in her throat it was as if she coughed up stones. That she flew down the steps to stop just short of the African in the dust. That slowly then, as if unsure, she just traced the scarifications graved like a cat's face into the African face. That each met the gaze of the last person with whom she could converse. That—but how can I speak for her, whose name would again be lost?—they embraced.

3

Give Us

This Day

The Infusion Room

Mercy on Maryanne who through a hole beneath her collarbone drinks
   the life-preserving fluid, while in her arm
another IV tube drips something green. "It never affects me," she says,
   "I'm fortunate."
She has Crohn's and rheumatoid arthritis and now osteoporosis, as well as
   no gamma globulin
as we all have no gamma globulin, or at least not enough. Mercy on Aaron,
her son, who at fifteen has Hodgkins and arthritis and no gamma
   globulin, who is out of school
just for the moment. "He's so bright," the doctor says, "he'll make it up."
   But of course
you never (as I remember) quite make it up. (Sitting up all night so as not
   to cough,
coughing so hard I tore the cartilage off three ribs. "If I was God," the
   then-doctor said,
"I'd design better ribs.")

Mercy on Mitzi who shook for three hours the first day I was there, and
   Cynthia
who cried because of the pain in her legs but aspires to horseback riding.
"Mitzi's tough," the nurse said admiringly, and I thought, could I ever be
   so tough?
Could I wear a velvet cap like Cynthia? Mitzi's on chemo.

And mercy on Paul, who drives a cab part-time and has sores on his
   ankles.
"If you could put your feet up more," the doctor suggests. He winces as
   she touches his skin, explains
if he could just finish college he could get a better job, but to finish college
   he has to drive this cab,
and I think of my luck all those years teaching at a college, the flexible
   hours, pleasant rooms

where you could always put your feet up if need be. Mercy on Mike,
the pilot, who looks like a jockey, who shows us pictures of his
    14-month-old girl,
who used to be allergic, as I am allergic, so that now while Mike reads
    the comics,
his friend leans against the wall, thumbing a computer manual, faithful,
    a tad overweight.
Mercy on the wholesale grocer, the man who sells prostheses, the
    used-Caddy salesman moving to glossy Florida,
the one who says candidly, "The first two days of each week are OK,
    then I begin to get tired."

Mercy on the black kid strapped to his Walkman, mercy on all like
    him who fall asleep.
Mercy on Sally Jessy Raphael and the interminable talk show flickering
    down the morning as we drift, or shiver, or sleep.
Aaron puts his huge sneakers up on Maryanne's seat and she holds
    his hand lightly while he sleeps;
they look like the Creation of Adam.

            2

I think if you could see us now we'd resemble giant grasshoppers
whose skinny elbows vibrate slightly above their heads, or I think
    that the room

if you approached it by space ship would look like a busy harbor,
crammed with barges, their curious cargo, and cranes extended or at
    half mast,

but all functional, needed. The TV twitters. The nurses are taking a
    break
from the hard business of giving us each day (at two- or three- or
    four-week intervals)

our daily, habitable lives. We too could go on a talk show,
challenging truckers' wives, twins who have lost their Other. I peel open
   my sandwich

with my good, unencumbered right hand. The IV poles gleam, we float
   on our black recliners.
It is almost time for the soaps.

The Children's Ward

Nanny was Irish, I told my mother, *born* in Scotland. Her sister was Head of Ladies' Ready To Wear at the biggest shop in Greenoch. Her oldest sister that was, there were nine in the family. The youngest of all was Our Joseph, not much older than me, and when the little princesses visited Greenoch, Nanny went to see them, along with all the other people lining the streets, but they couldn't hold a candle to Our Joseph. Nanny took care of me because once before she had taken care of a little boy who was sick the same way I was. So she understood my diet. "Poor wee thing," she would say and tell how one day somebody brought her a box of chocolates and the boy took some, which of course he wasn't supposed to do, and when he heard her coming he sat down on the box and squashed the chocolates flat. But when she caught me lifting icing off my sister's birthday cake, I was spanked. "This hurts me more than it does you," Nanny would say, her wrists like steel, while I screamed. Yet she looked back on that boy with tenderness. "Poor wee lamb"—and she explained how with the disease we had you were supposed to die before you were seven. "And did he die, Nanny? Is he dead now?" But I never found out.

Curds without whey—four times a day Nanny put the junket through the ricer and squeezed it dry—bananas, the lean of bacon, protein milk that tasted like chalk. I was standing holding up my glass and crying. I cried all the time now, every morning playing with the other children I would start to cry. My grandmother's stylish heels clicked across the floor. "Here Junebug, it's not as bad as all that, I'll show you." She took a gulp, puckered up her lips and rushed out into the hall. Nanny handed the glass back to me. "Drink up," she said, out of patience. "If you don't drink your milk like a good girl, we'll be planting daisies on your grave by August."

There was a woman in their town who lost all five sons in the War, and when the Armistice came and they had the big parade, she closed her window shades and refused to watch. I imagined how that house looked, small, between two taller houses, with black shades. I liked the stories about Our Joseph better. And how they all slept together in the one big bed. I used to wake up early and see Nanny lying in the other half of our bed, her nose pointing to the ceiling, her firm chest rising and falling under the saint's medal and small gold cross. "When Father says *turn*," she would command, "we all turn."

God knew Nanny would have saved my life if she could, but since there was apparently no saving it, she did her duty. Her duty was to see I didn't die any sooner than I had to and make sure I got to Heaven when I did die. So I had A CHILD'S TALES FROM THE BIBLE, in red and gold, every night and "The Catholic Hour" over the radio on Sundays. All day I looked forward to bedtime. My favorite was Moses in the Bulrushes. Fancy finding a live baby floating in a nest down our river, the way Pharaoh's Daughter had! But I hated Abraham. In the picture he held the knife over Isaac's head and Isaac looked terrified; the ram bleated in the bushes. When I had been really sick, lying on my back in bed with a swollen stomach, someone brought Harriet to visit me. Harriet was three, a year younger than me. Over the curve of my huge stomach, I could just see her wedged between the foot of the bed and the wall. She was carrying a present for me but was too scared to budge. After she had gone Nanny said, "Harriet's a Jew." "What's a Jew?" I said. "They're God's chosen people." A few days later I announced, "I'm going to be a Jew." "You can't"—Nanny stopped folding—"you have to be born one." "Can't I ever?" I thought about Harriet's curls and dark, reproachful eyes. She was the most beautiful child I had ever seen. I wanted to be chosen more than anything.

"You have to learn to read now you're five because I learned to read when I was five," said Isabel importantly. I was squeezed into the old highchair because I liked looking down on things; no one used it any more. "No, I don't," I said, "nobody has to learn to read till they're six." At eight, Pen was still learning. Besides, I didn't want to keep growing older this way. The other children raced up and down the room. Nanny burst in, her hands still red from the soapsuds. "There," she declared, plucking me out of the highchair, "can't you see you've gone and made Jane cry again?" "I didn't, I didn't," protested Isabel, "you're unfair." "Don't be impertinent," said Nanny—she pronounced it im-*pair*tinent. In her arms I was crying harder, leaning my head into her white, starched shoulder. Pen and Isabel must hate me. Even when the circus came to town, on its way north from winter quarters, they might not get to go for fear they'd bring home another germ.

But the first night I got sick Pen had been excited. We were in our small summer house then, where I used to stand up in my crib to watch the mountains and the long black freight train hooted out of its tunnel in the clear evening light. I was perched on the toilet; a bare lightbulb burned against the wall. Pen danced across the bathroom, shrieking and laughing. "There goes the King!" he shrieked. "There goes the Queen!" That was an old game we had, whenever a bad thunderstorm hit. Pen played chess, and he liked to pretend the thunder was giant chessmen falling off the board of Heaven and rolling around on the ground. But tonight the thunder was my farts. Bent over on the toilet seat, queasy and trembling, I hurt with laughter because of Pen. My brother's wiry body flashed by. A shadow jerked up the wall. "There goes the Queen!" I shouted wildly. "There goes a pawn!"

Then I was lying in bed with my stomach puffed so high I couldn't bear to sit up even against pillows. I hurt all the time. My mother read THE WATER BABIES. Every time she got to the last page and shut the book I would demand to hear it over again, right from the beginning. Poor Tom, dirty and miserable, sank underneath the river and the whole husk of his body was washed away, and soon he was clean and shining, no bigger than Daddy's thumb. My father blocked the light in the bedroom door. We stared at each other. Then the doorway was empty, he had left without saying anything. "He can't stand to see anybody sick," said my mother to my aunt, in a voice I wasn't supposed to catch. My aunt began to sing to me so my mother could go lie down. Far away the black freight train hooted. "She'll be comin' round the mountain when she comes," sang my aunt.

When we finally traveled north it was on a long black train. We had a drawing room on the Southern Railway. The trip took two nights and a day. I sat with my legs straight out in front of me and looked out the window. Every once in a while I would push the green plush of the train seat the wrong way—dark-light, dark-light; then I would peer around at my mother. What should I talk to her about? For months I had been with almost no one but Nanny.

2

Every Sunday the two of us would dress to go to Mass. Under the tent of her white cotton nightgown Nanny would mysteriously draw on first her underclothes, then her long, best silk stockings. Then over the top went her best striped silk dress, and the nightgown fell down in a little puddle at her feet. She fastened the neck of the dress with a cameo brooch, slipping the medal and gold cross inside. Then she would dress me. Daddy would drop us off on his way to his own church, where he was a vestryman. By this time I had a medal of my own—St. Teresa, carrying a sheaf of lilies. The Little Flower was Nanny's special saint. That was her middle name, Teresa, after Bessie. Nanny had said I could have St. Teresa for my special saint, too.

Out of respect for St. Paul, Nanny always wore a dark, short-brimmed felt hat which she pulled down almost to the tops of her fiercely blue eyes. I had to wear a bonnet with a snap under the chin that scratched. At the door of the church she would dip her fingers in the scalloped shell over my head and cross my forehead with holy water. The water dropping into the stone shell made a pleasant tinkling sound.

I loved the inside of that church. It was large and dark, like a cave, and you couldn't say anything, but still it was always warm with the rustle of skirts and prayer-book pages and the low groans of old men getting up off their knees. As Nanny leaned forward to pray, I would look up at the reds and blues of the stained-glass windows or try to find through the rows of bodies the pink dress of the plaster saint stretching out her hand from the side aisle. Then the priest would start to chant, little bells would ring, and the church would fill up with the smells of all the different people and the stuffy, interesting smell of incense shaken out by a boy. Above me Nanny's profile was stern but not angry, and I knew she was praying for her brothers and sisters at home, for her father who never made more than two pounds ten a week, and also for the young man she had come over to this country to meet. He had paid her way out, but as soon as she saw him standing on the dock she knew they could never marry. So she went back to being a nanny. The priest in his gold or green or purple cape lifted his hands to the sky. Before him on the altar was a large gold cross. At home we had a black cross with a twisted Jesus hanging over the bed where we slept; there were nails through His feet and the blood ran down, and on His head was the crown of thorns.

One day the side aisle was crowded with children. Their mothers were trying to line them up two by two and making shushing noises. The boys had on dark blue suits, some even wore long pants, but I couldn't take my eyes off the girls. They were dressed in white, like little brides, and on their heads were white veils fastened with wreaths of daisies or wax orange blossoms. Each one carried a bouquet in a white paper ruffle just like a real bride. Nanny had a friend in Greenoch who became a nun—bride of Christ, she called her. Were these the brides of Christ? "Wouldn't you like to make your first Communion?" whispered Nanny. "But you have to be seven. The age of reason," she added practically.

Nanny took the hairbrush to me. "This hurts me more than it does you," she was almost crying. I had been standing by the ironing board. "Go to the bathroom, Jane," she said. But I wouldn't go. And then I couldn't hold it in any longer, shameful and brown it poured down my legs. The hairbrush hissed through the air. I got down off the bed again stiffly.

I hated Abraham. *Dis*obedient! proclaimed Nanny. But was it Abraham's fault or God's? How could God ask Abraham to kill his only son if He loved him? And how could God let His own Son die? I stared and stared at the twisted Jesus hanging over Nanny's side of the bed. There were nails through His hands, too.

In Isabel's room hung the picture of Paradise. Little boys and girls in yellow and red and blue dresses were standing holding flowers, while lambs and rabbits and sparrows played about their feet. "He prayeth best who loveth best," Isabel read to me from the borders, "All things both great and small." On Pen's wall was the face of a tiger, coming out from among reeds at a water hole in Africa. I never went into Pen's room now if I could help it.

My sins were crying, lying and not wanting to go to the bathroom. "Don't touch yourself, Jane," Nanny pursed up her lips in disgust. One day she said to me, "If you don't stop touching yourself, we'll have to take you to the hospital and get it cut off." I screamed with terror. For a long time I wouldn't stop screaming. Nanny still had all her own teeth. And she had a right to feel proud of them, they were so white. "Soot and salt," she declared—who could afford toothpaste? Their father had taught them all to reach right up the chimney. I watched her smile in fascination. How could anything so white come from anything so dirty as the fireplace? Was this what the priest meant when he said our sins would be washed whiter than snow?

Nanny went up to Communion. She always did that, leaving me alone in the dark wooden pew. But today I felt tired. The people shuffling back down the aisles seemed farther away than usual; the murmur of their prayers was like the sound of the river out our dark bedroom windows on a still winter's night. Nanny was bending over me. My face was cold with sweat. "You fainted," she said with concern. I was surprised to find myself lying in the pew as if it was our bed; a man's jacket lay across my knees. "Poor wee lamb." Daddy came to fetch us, looking worried. Tenderly she carried me out to the car. But after that I couldn't go to church any more, I could only have the Bible stories at bedtime.

"Jane, Jane, Go to Spain, And never come home again!" they chanted at a birthday party. But would I go to Heaven or Hell? I felt very tired. I was standing beside the table where the others were already eating their ice cream and angel food cake. At my place was a bowl of curds.

It was the Depression. But fortunately Nanny's mother had always been a good manager. When nobody else ate liver, she got it off the butcher for dog scraps and they all made a good meal. Not one of them had ever missed a day at school or on the job because of illness. With relish Nanny told how her older sister lost her first post in the hat department in Glasgow. "What you need, madam," Agnes talked back to the customer, "is not a new hat, it's a new face."

Even though it was the Depression, we could still have our new Easter dresses. Mine was to be yellow, with baskets of flowers on a white path down the front. But to wear it, I had to get through the Crucifixion. "Away in a manger, No crib for His bed," we had sung at Christmastime. Now Jesus was the Lamb of God caught by His horns in the bushes. He was betrayed and whipped and they mocked Him and hung Him on the cross saying, "This is the King of the Jews." And they gave Him vinegar to drink. And after He was dead one of the soldiers pierced His side with a spear, and blood and water ran out. And doubting St. Thomas had to thrust his hand into Our Lord's side to make sure He was risen. How could he do that?

All during Lent we read these stories about Jesus. Nanny had no use for people who gave up things for Lent, like my grandmother. When you were really poor, she said, what was left to give up? It was better to show devotion.

I woke up crying. Nanny fussed a bit but brought the water. Then she climbed back into bed and turned her shoulder on me, so as to get back to sleep. I watched the white mound of her body in the thin crack of light from the bathroom door and listened to the slap-slap of the river against the pilings below the house. How could God let His only Son die? And how could Jesus, if He loved me, possibly let me die and go to Hell? After all I was only a child. I tried not to think of the face of the tiger gleaming through the dark from Pen's wall. At any moment he might bare his fangs. Other little animals came down to the water hole, Pen said, and the tiger lay in wait for them.

But suppose there was no Hell? How could God send anybody to Hell if He loved them? Jesus even loved the thief on the next cross. I was almost asleep now. I decided God couldn't have created Hell, there was no room for it.

On Easter morning the sun shone beautifully. Isabel and Pen and I put on our new clothes and were driven through the white streets to our grandparents' house for the big Easter dinner. "Like a picked chicken," one of the uncles said, seeing me in my yellow dress. But Nanny told me I looked a picture. Seated on the high cushion facing my glass of protein milk, I felt high and far away above the rest of the table. The sun shone in on the colors of their new dresses and newly washed hair. Jesus loved me. But today it hardly mattered. For if everybody bad and good went to Heaven, what was the point of being good? There was no Heaven. You died, and that was that.

3

"Take her north to a doctor you can trust. She's dying, and you're dying watching her." That's the way my mother told the story to my aunt, after my father brought home the first real cash he'd been paid in over a year and laid it on the dresser. Never had he worked so hard, complained my mother, but it was because everybody was going bankrupt. We were in Schwartz's toy store. I couldn't make up my mind between a doll with a whole trunk full of clothes and a cardboard village that had a church, a town hall with a star over the front door, a castle, and a lot of horses, sheep and pigs. Finally my mother said I could keep them both. I couldn't believe it. At home we almost never had new toys. Back in the hotel bedroom she helped me pile up the pillows to make snow-capped mountains. On the top peak stood the castle, down below was the church, and on the green blankets over my knees I arranged the little cardboard houses where people really lived, which I liked best of all. But I still couldn't think what to talk to her about. There were three men and three women in that village. One of the women had no hair and a very red face. She looked bossy, and I decided she had no children of her own. She could take care of the pigs.

The nurse in the waiting room called me "she," though I was standing right there. "But she didn't cry," the nurse kept saying stubbornly to my mother, turning the white-rimmed barium glass round and round in her fingers. "Are you sure you didn't just pour it out? They always cry."

He was not stooping or kneeling down to be at my level. Instead he had put his large square hands under my naked armpits and lifted me up to stand on the examining table. From where I stood I could look directly into his blue eyes. He had white curls all over his head, and I thought that was why he was called Dr. Kerley. Naked, I regarded him with trust. "You know," he said at once, "you're going to be all right." How could he understand all that I had felt? He told me before he told my mother.

4

My mother didn't want to leave me alone on the ward but I was delighted. Every day while we shared the small room at the hospital I would creep down to the end of the hall and peer in at the ward door and wonder about the children who lived there. Those children were old campaigners. They could tell the names of the various diseases and how they affected you. Frances, for instance, was an epileptic. That meant you fell down in fits. Frances was very pretty, and I used to love to lie and watch her still profile through the thin cheesecloth curtain that at rest hour divided our two cots. She had long, pale braids, and when she sat up they slid silkily down her back. Frances was almost nine and rarely smiled. After a while I decided she would not get better. You could usually tell.

For over a year I had weighed 42 pounds. Because of the diet my second teeth might not come in with enamel. But I didn't have celiac disease, all I had to do was stay in the hospital and learn how to eat again. Dr. Kerley stood at the foot of my cot, my mother was perched on the side. But I wouldn't look up. I was holding the brimming spoonful so that it sparkled under the bedside bulb. It was my first real supper—cornflakes, with sweet, thin cow's milk.

The nurses on our ward never felt sorry for anyone. That was what was grand about them, they treated us just like ordinary children. Every morning at 6:30 they would wake us by switching on the harsh overhead lights and wiping our faces with grainy washcloths soaked in cold water. Then we had to wait a long time before they brought up breakfast. "Happy birthday, Jane!" announced the chief nurse, setting down across my knees with a thump a tray that had a green cardboard cake on it. Out of the cake came a sunburst of yellow ribbons, and at the end of each ribbon was a small green box. At last I was six. I turned my shoulder on the rest of the ward. Secretly I opened the first box. Inside was a tiny wooden tea set with red trim. As I balanced the long line of cups and plates down the longer line of my sheeted leg, I pretended they were overflowing with chocolate ice cream, cornflakes and angel food. That night I asked the nurse please to tie up all my presents again, so I could have the same birthday tomorrow morning.

The baby with tubes lay on one side of the hall door and Billy was on the other. They were the youngest children on the ward. Billy was only two and a half. The baby slept most of the time, and the tubes curled out from under his white knitted crib blanket and fell in a red garland to the floor. It was rumored he had kidney trouble. My cot was in the far corner, safe between Frances and the wall.

Once a week we were taken up on the roof to listen to stories. There we would be joined by groups of children from other wards, and crippled children would be wheeled in by their nurses in special chairs or carried on portable beds. It was sunny and crisp on the roof, and as you stepped out of the elevator you could see a great sweep of sky, blocks of apartment buildings with a few trees down below, and in the distance the glittering river that was still not as wide as our own river at home in Jacksonville. The storyteller wore a long, flowing robe and had an unusually sweet voice, and we would all sit or lie or stand listening while she recited fairy tales and sometimes sea gulls or a pigeon flew by overhead. My favorite was Boots and His Brothers, where the third child that everyone thinks is stupid grows up to win the princess by kindness or good luck.

One day when we came down off the roof and were crowding through the ward door, we discovered the baby had been taken away. His crib looked flat and white, and the bunch of red tubing was gone from underneath. "Gone for an operation," said the brisk young nurse who was folding his crib blanket. But he never came back. We all knew he must have died, though someone argued he could just have been put in a private room because he was so sick. Soon his place was taken by a cheerful girl with one leg in traction. They had run out of bed space in the bone and joint pavilion downstairs.

"Nurse-ah. Nurse-ah. Nurse-ah." The whole place smelt like a zoo. There was the smell of fear, the warm animal smell of sleeping bodies, and the sharp stink of hospital disinfectant coming up from the floor and the sheets. Billy had started it. He had waked up wanting the nurse and no one was on duty. She must just have stepped down the hall. By the time I woke up, everybody was shouting or crying. The ward was almost dark, and it took me a few moments to make out Billy clinging to the bars of his crib and beating on the top rail with his fist. Billy couldn't talk clearly yet and he was shrieking in panic. Nobody could get over the bars of their own beds to help him. I sat up, then I stood and leaned over the high end of my bed and kicked at the bottom railing with my bare foot. We all began to pound the rails with our hands. The smell grew heavier. Gradually a rhythm was pounded out, and together we began to shout as loud as we could for Billy: "*Nurse*-ah! *Nurse*-ah! *Nurse*-ah!" At last we could see flashlights coming down the hall, sending slanted shadows toward the ceiling as they got closer. Then the overhead lights glared on, and three nurses started fussing through the ward, telling the children to lie down and tucking us in with strict tightness. One of them picked up Billy, who was soaked through. Almost at once he fell asleep with his head on her shoulder. But I couldn't sleep for a long time, thinking of how we had all called together to save Billy.

I fell in love with George. George was a tall, well-built boy of seven, with a fleshy jaw and brown hair that started straight up from his forehead. All that was wrong with him was that he was waiting for another operation on his harelip. We were two of the well ones now, and every day we spent a lot of time together on the sun porch, building towers out of blocks, eating jello at a low table, or chasing each other around the room. "Be quiet, Jane. Now do be quiet, George," the nurses had to say, as we laughed and scuffled. Once they even had to separate us while we were wrestling, pulling George off from on top of me by the back of his blue shirt collar. Another day George was sitting in the big red fire engine pedaling hard and I was sitting on the back and he drove straight through the ward where our cots were and out the door to the hall and ran into the legs of Dr. Kerley. We ricocheted off the wall then, and both of us fell out laughing. When my mother came to visit, she was shocked to find I had learned to talk just like George. That was harelip language. There were hardly any consonants, only animal noises, and the lilt of true sentences running up and down. George and I always talked that way. It was our secret code to fool the nurses.

It was getting cold. Soon it would be time to go home. My mother came to visit, bringing with her a pair of brown leather leggings outgrown by my northern cousins. She got permission to take me for a walk outside the hospital, and together we set off down the strange city streets. At home I was used to grass and trees, so I stared at the gray, flashing pavements. Then I was leaning against an iron railing, looking down on ranks of boys in gray uniforms who marched and gestured rapidly with their hands. My mother kneeled down next to me and took my body in her arms. "They're deaf and dumb boys, darling," she said. "It's the deaf and dumb school. Those poor boys can't hear anything, and so they have to learn to talk with their fingers." I examined her face in surprise. Her eyes had blurred with tears. Then I pulled away a little and slipped one hand out of its glove, experimentally. It certainly was a cold day not to be able to wear gloves. I looked down at the boys again where they wheeled and beckoned without a sound from across their paved field. But didn't she know we all had something?

4

Vocation:

A Life

The Winter Road

. . . they have passed into the world as
abstractions, no one seeing what they are
    —GEORGIA O'KEEFFE *(1887–1986)*

I

Late winter light

Suppose it comes from the snow
blowing all day across your winter road
umber with violet shadows

Or suppose it comes from some energy farther away
that may never be understood
to keep us from repetition
from reciting the litany of loss

The last uncoupling of the galaxies—
how can that be understood?

You stand on a ridge facing silence
You lift your brush

2

Curve of an arm
Ripple of muscles down extended back
Rib cage of cliffs

The eye lays bare the muscle-rows of speech
the prehistoric arteries

It can all be told in color and light and line

Only recompose
the original soft palaver of the earth
        earth red   earth orange   earth purple
        pale Naples yellow   ochres
        even the soft earth greens

Clarify

Or take this "Fragment of the Ranchos de Taos Church," its
Mediterranean statement
        blue of the Isles
        calm butte   archaic thigh

3

Blue
Blue curtains opening on a gray sky
"Black Rock with Blue"
"Sky Above Clouds"

After all men's destruction has been honed away
by the winds that wrap the stars
still there will be blue

Half-blind you go on painting
in a blue smock

And the road past your house
              exaltation of a pear!
carves out the socket
of a hill, then orbits clean off the canvas
bound for *Espanola, Santa Fe and the world*

always there, always going away

tireless calligraphy
on snow without horizon

4

Where I have been
Where I have been is of no importance
To live to be a hundred is of no importance
only *what I have done* with it
              But we love the particular

Where I was born
Where I was born is of no importance
              torn shoe, nursing mouth, patchwork-cushioned chair
              still rocking quietly in the light wind
              of a late summer evening of some life

Nor *how I have lived*
with a handful of rocks
a wooden bodhisattva in a niche
a black door
and the continuous great adventure of the sky

Only what I have made of it
what I have been able to finish
To live to be a hundred is of no importance
This landscape is not human
I was meant to take nothing away

Vocation: A Life
Suite Based on Four Words
from Willa Cather

1. Desire

> *... too strong to stop, too sweet to lose ...*
> —THE SONG OF THE LARK

1915 It begins in indolence
It begins as a secret intelligence rising like a tune,
opening with the pores
It begins in secret
Thea lies on a rock-shelf, face to the sun,
eyelids closed against sun, the sun roaring
through her ears and pores. Before her a *river of ... air*
drops three hundred feet, behind her the cliff-house
—a tawny hollow—clings like a swallow's nest
The rock is smooth and warm and above all clean

The rock is above all clean
The Ancient People left no wounds in the earth
but a curious aspiration—a carbon stain
on the rock-roof above a cookfire, turkey bones,
the shard of a pot with a serpent's head in red,
a black water jar
where a woman blazed identical pale cliff-houses

A timid, nest-building folk?

No, the swallows live out their lives in a *wash of air*
The rock-shelf holds its heat
long after the canyon below has died into night

It begins as survival

Thea has died to her self, she is reborn
only as a vessel. Climbing the water trail
from the base of the canyon, she is *feet and knees and loins,*

a baby hangs to her back, on her head is a jar
of *sovereign* water, for healing. In simplest health
like a gold lizard on the rock-face, she climbs, dreams,
wakes in her cave
to the pulse of a tribal drumbeat,
the cicadas' anonymous drone

Everything drops away
and is reborn as energy. Like a spring
the monotonous tune wells in her throat all day
It has *nothing to do with words,* it is not a complaint
but more like the flex of a muscle. She grows young,
she is older than her mothers. Neediness,
neediness: our first speech
water   fire   seeds
throbs and fades on the solitude forever

But the old stream runs away
heartless
geological
sacred
as its idle lights pick out the canyon floor

Thea is only a *guest.* Bathing in her pool
at the foot of the canyon, among rosy and ochre stones,
screened by the cottonwoods' flicker, she is stunned
for a moment, to sculpture, lifting a huge sponge
halfway to her flushed shoulders. Here it begins:
With her throat could she . . . ? With their jars did they
catch the headlong, *shining . . . element?*
Women coiled the clay, women smoothed the colors. Song
dances on her breath, a ball on a column of air

Now everything takes the curve
of a *desire for action,* of a
brilliancy of motion. She
crouches in the bed of the stream

The shards of ceremony glisten
from that bed
in a crack
of the world

2. ROMANCE

*Oh, I didn't know anything! . . . But . . . when I set out from
Moonstone . . . , I had had a rich, romantic past*

—*THEA*

1909 Down by the Republican or Little Blue
six boys spend the night on a sandbar
They build their fire
on a *new bit of world,* a tiny beach
where fish and turtle bones
tell over again the legend of evolution
It's all a retelling
in the frank, frontier speech of Nebraska
of a ghost story by Turgenev
Only here the boys are talking of Coronado
not of the water-goblin, how he reached
this very river maybe, how he died
        always afraid of *dying in a cornfield*
      Red Cloud   Pittsburgh   New York
simplified by his dream. . . .
A bobcat leaps, a whooping crane
screams in this virgin tale
of mound builders, cliff-dwellers, till the "Enchanted Bluff"
rears out of a homely, imagined desert
with all her dead on board

      Mesa Encantada!
Your reserve blocks my view like a rock

1893 Who could never forget the summer the corn scorched in the ear
Who could never forget how the immigrant farmers went bankrupt
they were sold up, they took to the roads, they took their own lives
a few went crazy at home
Who wrote by night for a dollar a column and studied by day

in your garish hat, in your too-thin coat
Imperious

> *Write ordinary life as though it were history*
> *. . . so as to make us dream*

But one must have simple tastes—to give up a good salary

What it must have cost you, in your red-embroidered Liberty gown
Throw all the furniture out of the window!

What it must have cost you
        not, after all, the Seven Golden Cities
        London   Paris   Bayreuth
        but the past in a crack of the past

  Walnut Canyon, Arizona, spring of 1912

> *for I shall be the first, if I live,*
> *to bring the Muse into my country*

Dreamer, you were almost forty
when you finally saw the Southwest

1918 It was always there
        Like an old tune out of childhood or country refrain
        played over again to four homesick girls
        in MY ÁNTONIA, years later, the design was there:
        Sandtown   Moonstone   Black Hawk
        the failure of Coronado
        and the child extravagantly reading
        by the star of her railroadman's lantern
        at an open window

3. POSSESSION

> *... the design of his life had been the work of this secondary social man, the lover*
>
> —PROFESSOR ST. PETER

> *For me the mesa was no longer an adventure. . . . It was possession*
>
> —TOM OUTLAND, THE PROFESSOR'S HOUSE

1925 To begin
with the window
as an element of design:
       sonata form
       Cervantes' tale-within-a-tale
       that square open window
       giving on the sea
       (In the work of the old Dutch masters, though the foreground
         is full
       of red-patterned carpets, copper vessels, bedsteads, ripe fruit,
       still the girl pouring wine, in the sun, if she looks up
       has a map
       no, an actual view
       of masts "like a forest in winter"
       and the steel-gray   wealthy   or is it empty now?
       untranslatable sea)
Q. What's left for the mature artist but an examination of method?
A. *It is only the practised hand that can make the natural gesture,—and the practised hand has often to grope its way*

To begin again
in America:
       a blue, hazy smear
          the Blue Mesa!
       his *inland sea*
          a *naked blue rock!*
       the Lake

of the Professor's landlocked childhood
just glimpsed from his attic
      Tom Outland's
      unsolved landmark
But suppose it is all a mistake

THE PROFESSOR'S HOUSE is a novel about property

Even the Professor's books have been turned into property
      "Histories," he calls them
      History? a
romance . . . of the imagination! Off the coast of Spain
once he'd gazed up at the snow-peaks, unfolding rose
from a matrix of purple water, fading to gold
toward the West of El Dorado. . . .
And the design was sound, he could trust it, *it had seen him through*
He is fifty-two
with nothing left to write or to love
but the journal of a poor dead cowhand,
vibrating and austere
If words . . . cost money, he thinks,
they might taste this pure

The Professor as Coronado?

So it wasn't the War
The world broke in two in 1922 or thereabouts
      suicide?
         celibacy?
            thereabouts?

THE PROFESSOR'S HOUSE is a novel with two heroes
      two possible endings
      two lovers, unacknowledged,

of the same sex
            a third lover
and in 1923 Isabelle McClung, securely married,
offered you the perfect studio annexed to her French house

He had never learned to live without delight

Even the Professor's women are creatures of property
            not Thea   Alexandra   Ántonia
            classical as jars
            but a "bust" or a "birdcage." The *social . . . bond*
            makes them dressmakers' dummies. To breathe "I love"
            in a world of acquisition, to blurt out "I trust"
            is to lie on a bosom of sawdust
            and fall
                        to face a sour wall
                        What were you doing on Park Avenue
                        in your last apartment, viewless and vast,
                        away from the roar?
(In MY ÁNTONIA, how everything swells and subsides quite naturally
in our lost out-of-doors)

THE PROFESSOR'S HOUSE *is . . . the most personal of Willa Cather's
novels,* wrote valiant Edith Lewis; therefore, not autobiographical

                        unless the light comes from some faraway place
                        unless the source of light is beyond ourselves
                        unless we become ourselves
                        increasingly
The pioneer plot had failed you
In 1923 they gave you the Pulitzer Prize for the wrong book
But weren't you now a famous, indeed a wealthy woman?

What it must have cost you
     And this gift of sympathy is [the writer's] *great gift*
to deal, finally, with coldness at heart

                    sonata form, or
                    the story of a shipwreck
               yet the key changes
               as the original theme speaks:

solitary

Whenever Tom enters the mesa he is solitary
Whether from the canyon he looks up, through the falling snow,
to a round red tower, asleep, a city asleep
high on the cliff-face, veiled, in the lavender air
—a cluster of human remains still undisturbed—
or whether he returns just at sunset as the gold dies away
from his plundered birthright, to find it, after all, whole
and the arc of evening sky whole
and the distant stars whole
as they always have been—till now?—he is at home
on earth, alone,
simplified

not possessing but
possessed

4. UNFURNISHING

There was an element of exaggeration in anything so simple!
—*DEATH COMES FOR THE ARCHBISHOP*

1927 Upon this rock
          Ácoma
          Mont Réal
Upon this rock I shall
          scaffolding   sailing
          bearing the ghost of the church in its *ship of . . . air*
          unburdening
Under the myriad broad galactic stare
Out of this yellow rock
Out of this clay, stuff of the planet's veins
Out of my body I build my
          but not to be mistaken for death

Whatever is felt upon the page without being specifically named there,—
that, one might say, is created

1943 So the poor singer with painful, broken wrists,
the rich young fellow whose tongue has been torn out,
reveal one aging writer, her hand in a splint,
unable to dictate
having lost the pure thrust from throat to page

And this is all we know of your last novel, HARD PUNISHMENTS, left
unfinished at your death and destroyed according to your will

Before that, a sort of litany:
          OBSCURE DESTINIES
        SHADOWS ON THE ROCK
      DEATH COMES FOR THE ARCHBISHOP

the gift of tongues
in a clean adobe room
only the shadows
violet . . .

It begins again
as a miracle, that is
a change in perception

I feel as if I had been journeying over the rim of the world
for ten years: October to October
You have *teased* [my] *mind*
and this is *sympathy*. Last night as low gray clouds
drove rapidly across a raw, towering sunset
like the scooped-out wall of a canyon seen from below,
I stood in a meadow near Jaffrey, invoking two crows
to fly from here to the gravesite. Edith lies at your feet
On your stone is chiseled . . . THAT IS HAPPINESS: TO BE DISSOLVED
INTO SOMETHING COMPLETE AND GREAT   The next words
ring only in silence: *When it comes to one, it comes*
as naturally as sleep

When we try to sum up a lifetime, events cease to matter
just as, in the end, a novel's
plot does not matter
What we came away with was never written down
Vibration, overtone, timbre, a fragrance as distinct
as that of an old walled garden . . . *The text is not there—*
but something was there, all the same, some intimacy,
all that is needed
in a vigorous, rich speaking voice

[Your] *secret?*
It is every artist's secret. Your secret
was *passion*

The singer, the professor, the religious
—three motifs I understand—
and the child
But my motifs are not my subject, cried the painter,
my subject is

How the *vehemence of the sun suggested motion!*

1927
Like Don Quijote and Sancho, they are always on the move,
the two padres. The Bishop is alone
in a wilderness of red sand-hills
Or together they slog among the Truchas, lead-purple under rain
Or the Bishop approaches the pueblos, white, ochre, sullen rose,
through a sandstorm, under starlight. He is drowning in snow
but is saved by his young Pecos guide. With his Navajo friend
he is riding through *blue . . . stinging air,*
tossed by the shadows of a cloudscape, monotonous and free

without ownership, without scar
of European conquest or dreams

Here the earth was never a *second body*
but only the *floor of the sky*

Artistic growth is, more than it is anything else, a refining of the sense of
truthfulness

glimpse of a dooryard, glimpse of the South:
acacia, with its *intense blue-green . . .*
colour of old paper window-blinds

touch and pass on

The Archbishop forgives himself everything, even his mistakes
were no more than *accidents.* He is outside time
Poverty, solitude
have strangely flowered. And the Indian
will survive—so he consoles himself
He who came with the buffalo has *lived to see*
the railroads . . . dreamed . . . across the mountains
Carnelian-fired hills
reach out to enfold his cathedral   Sangre de Cristo
rock of living gold
incomplete as friendship in action

I shall die of having lived

But nothing can take this away
Not according to my desires, but if it be for thy glory
supreme mirage of the flesh!

gold of a desert morning
light by which the writing
was composed

Notes

The Weather of Six Mornings

Originally, this book opened with the "March" sequence and closed with the title poem. I have rearranged the collection so that it follows a more chronological order. Four poems have been dropped. Seven have been added: "Letters" (first published in *Maps & Windows*); "Blind Girl" and "Roman Dream" (two of the "reclaimed" poems from *Scaffolding*); and, previously unpublished, "Snow in the City," "The Figure on the Far Side," "Iron," and "All the Leaves Were Green."

Page 64: "Feathers." The first line of "Feathers," like the sequence title "March," is taken from one of Zhivago's poems in Pasternak's *Doctor Zhivago* (poems translated by Bernard Guilbert Guerney).

Page 65: "Hunger Moon." In February 1967, the *New York Times* noted that, among Middle Western farmers, the last full moon before the spring equinox used to be called the "hunger moon" because there was not enough feed left in the barns for the animals, yet it was still too early to plant. However, it seems more likely that the phrase goes back to the Native Americans.

Page 66: "El Sueño de la Razón." A nightmare etching by Goya is inscribed "El sueño de la razón produce monstruos"—"The dream of reason begets monsters."

Page 70: "Middle Age." The line "Only the miracle is real" comes from Lukács but echoes much in Pasternak—for instance, "In real life, I thought, everything must be a miracle" (from *I Remember,* chapter on Scriabin).

Maps & Windows

Originally, this book opened with a small section of twenty "new and selected poems," under the title "Calling Me from Sleep." Eleven of these poems are now included in Part 3, "Dispossessions." After "Calling Me from Sleep" came "Nothing Has Been Used . . . ," then "Mercator's World." Again, I have opted for a more chronological arrangement here. One poem from the old "Mercator's World" has been dropped, one—"Song"—was added from *Scaffolding,* and one—"P.O.W."—is previously unpublished. In Part 3, "Messages" and "Holding Out" were first published in *Scaffolding,* while previously unpublished are "After the Blackout (1965)," "Dream in Which the Routine Quality of My Imagination Is Fully Exposed," and "95°."

Page 88: "After the Bomb Tests." Specifically, the United States tests at Bikini Atoll in the Marshall Islands, Western Pacific, 1946. Kepler (1571–1630) formulated the laws of planetary motion.

Page 95: "Nothing Has Been Used in the Manufacture of This Poetry That Could Have Been Used in the Manufacture of Bread." Throughout, Adrienne Rich's essay "When We Dead Awaken: Writing as Re-Vision" (1971), in *On Lies, Secrets, and Silence* (New York: Norton, 1979; reissued 1995), was in many ways central to my thinking.

Page 97: See Tillie Olsen's 1962 talk/essay, now reprinted as "Silences in Literature," at the beginning of her book *Silences.* Olsen lists the important women writers of the nineteenth century who never married and points to the surprisingly large number even in this century who have remained single or, at any rate, childless.

Page 97: John Berryman, *The Dream Songs,* number 187.

Page 104: "Now that we turn against the whole notion. . . ." How I wish "we" did! But I have not wanted to change the original course of this argument.

Page 109: Elizabeth Bishop has since become one of my necessary poets—as has Berryman.

Page 117: Anaïs Nin, *Diary of Anaïs Nin, 1934–39.* The whole passage reads: "Rank believes that to create it is necessary to destroy. Woman cannot destroy. He believes that may be why she has rarely been a great artist. In order to create without destroying, I nearly destroyed myself."

Page 129: "Cemetery in Pernambuco: Our Lady of Light." One of a series of poems by the contemporary Brazilian poet João Cabral de Melo Neto. Pernambuco is one of the poorest states in Brazil, and Cabral's concern is for the peasants, mostly sugarcane cutters, there.

Page 134: "Inheritances." Quoted virtually in its entirety from Rilke's *The Notebooks of Malte Laurids Brigge,* translated by M. D. Herter Norton (New York: Norton, 1992).

Scaffolding

This was a full-scale "new and selected poems," and eight of the nine "new" poems are included here ("Flute Song" has since been incorporated into "From the Journal Concerning My Father" in *Green Notebook, Winter Road*). In addition, "All These Dreams" has been transferred from *Scaffolding*'s "reclaimed poems" section. Previously unpublished in book form are "Scattered Words for Emily Dickinson," "S. Eliason 66: *Double Portrait of Emily Dickinson and the Rev. Charles Wadsworth,*" "Evening Star (Georgia O'Keeffe)," "Olympic Rain Forest," "Starting with a Line from Roethke," and "The River in All Lights, from an Upstairs Window."

Page 148: "*Evening Star.*" The quotation is from *Georgia O'Keeffe* by Georgia O'Keeffe.

Page 150: "Starting with a Line from Roethke." The line is from Theodore Roethke's "The Shape of the Fire."

Page 152: "Jittoku, Buddhist Mystic—15th Century." See, in the Boston Museum of Fine Arts, *Jittoku, a Buddhist Mystic, Laughing at the Moon* (school of Geiami, 1432–1485).

Page 156: "Praise." The image of stone as the poet's building material and the phrase about the world's being set free for our play during the two thousand years of Christian civilization are both taken from Osip Mandelstam, as reported by Nadezhda Mandelstam in *Hope Against Hope,* Chapter 56, "The Earth and Its Concerns." The chapter begins: "A woman who has come back after many years in the forced-labor camps tells me that she and her companions in misfortune always found comfort in the poetry which, luckily, she knew by heart and was able to recite to them. They were particularly moved by some lines M. wrote as a young man: *But I love this poor earth, because I have not seen another.*"

Page 158: "Threads." This poem is based on Rosa Luxemburg's *Prison Letters to Sophie Liebknecht,* the wife of her friend and co-revolutionary Karl Liebknecht. Together Rosa Luxemburg and Karl Liebknecht founded the Spartacus League and opposed the kaiser's war policy, and they spent almost the whole of World War I as political prisoners in various German prisons. Both were released a few days before the armistice, only to be picked up again by government authorities, interrogated, and killed. Rosa Luxemburg was beaten about the head, shot, and her body dumped in a canal. Her friend Hans Dieffenbach, a doctor, had been killed at the front. I am grateful to Independent Labour Publications, Leeds, U.K., for permission to quote from the *Prison Letters,* translated from the German by Eden and Cedar Paul.

Green Notebook, Winter Road

This book has been reproduced as it originally appeared, except for the insertion of four poems not previously published in book form: "Mourning Picture," "For the Recorder of Suicides," "Nothing I Meant To Keep," and "Mary Coldwell."

Page 181: "Mourning Picture." The italicized phrases come from the artist's catalog copy for this and another, untitled painting. Of "For John Berryman (1914–1972)" Eliason wrote: "When I read in January of Berryman's suicide leap from a Minneapolis bridge it was as if he would never stop falling and rock and stones (were there any?) changed to molten masses as unwritten poems, not to be lost, spilled everywhere, searing, dissolving the surrounding landscape. There is no color."

Page 185: "The Calling." Direct quotations are from Muriel Rukeyser's poem "The Outer Banks" and *The American Heritage Dictionary*. Reference is also made to an earlier poem, "Then I Saw What the Calling Was," and to Rukeyser's prose life of the Elizabethan navigator/explorer/astronomer *The Traces of Thomas Hariot*. Of this 350-page work she said (*New York Quarterly* [Summer 1972]), "The Hariot book is a footnote to the Outer Banks poem." She changed the last line of "The Outer Banks" as shown and described it as a breakthrough. On the back cover of *Hariot* is a close-up by Berenice Abbott of part of Rukeyser's eyebrow and one great eye.

Page 189: "Hotel de Dream." Cora Crane, the common-law wife of Stephen Crane, both before and after their literary life together in England, ran a bawdy house in Jacksonville called Hotel de Dream.

Page 203: "Being Southern." "Einstein *like a disembodied spirit*"—my father's words.

Page 205: "Seventeen Questions About KING KONG." I am indebted not only to repeated viewings of the film, but also, for general background information, to *The Making of King Kong,* by Orville Goldner and George E. Turner. I learned about Uncle Farmie's gift of *Explorations and Adventures in Equatorial Africa* from Ronald Haver's *David O. Selznick's Hollywood*. The last line of the poem was said to me in conversation.

Page 207: "Clementene." Muriel Rukeyser used often to ask groups, from elementary-school kids to middle-aged graduate students, to write a few lines beginning *I could not tell*. In our most secret conflicts, she believed, lie our inescapable poems.

Page 209: "How Can I Speak for Her?" I'm grateful to my cousin the late Nancy Osborne Bennett for tracing some of the historical material mentioned here, and to Judith Gleason for describing the look of certain Yoruba scarifications and repeating the sounds of the young girls' speech and songs.

Page 233: "The Winter Road." All quotations in italics are from *Georgia O'Keeffe* by Georgia O'Keeffe. Painting titles are in quotation marks except for "The Winter Road," which is referred to specifically in Part 3. I am indebted for several details in Part 3 to Eleanor Munro's *Originals: American Women Painters*.

Page 237: "Vocation: A Life." During one October spent in Iowa, I began to reread the works of Willa Cather, and it soon became clear to me that whenever she wrote about the Southwest, she was also writing about art. I have always loved serial paintings, such as Monet's waterlilies, where the same subject is studied again and again under different lights and in different weathers. In Cather's case, whenever she returned in imagination to the mesas and Anasazi cliff dwellings and clean skies over the desert, it seems she was pondering the mystery of vocation at a different lifetime stage. Thus Thea's sexual awakening in Panther Canyon (Walnut Canyon) in *The Song of the Lark* (1915) really marks her determination to go to Germany to become a singer. (Cather "was convinced that the great thing was *desire* in art"—Bennett.) And even before she herself first visited the Southwest—a visit that coincided with her final leave of absence from *McClure's Magazine* in order to write full-time—she had evoked the glowing image of the Mesa Encantada in a story about small-town Nebraska boys, "The Enchanted Bluff" (1909).

In *The Professor's House* (1925) Cather again evoked the mesa, this time the Blue Mesa (based on the actual Mesa Verde), as a sort of window opening out beyond all she most feared from a successful middle age: fame soured by lack of privacy, wealth that is not freedom but a product, sexual crisis, exhaustion of primary subject matter, bankruptcy of the national/colonial dream. (The professor's eight-volume history is a homage to the Spanish conquistadors.) By *Death Comes for the Archbishop,* written only two years later, we are released wholly into the landscape, but the landscape is postimpressionist, valedictory. The struggle is no longer in the present.

"Write ordinary life as though it were history . . . so as to make us dream" is my amalgam, freely translated, of two quotations from Flaubert that hung over the desk of Cather's friend and mentor, Sarah Orne Jewett. In a memorable letter of December 1908, Jewett counseled the younger woman: "The writer is the only artist who must be a solitary and yet needs the widest outlook upon the world." "For I shall be the first . . . to bring the Muse into my country" is of course Cather's own rendering of Virgil's lines from *My Ántonia.*

All other quotations are from works by or about Willa Cather—besides those already mentioned, *A Lost Lady* and Cather's essays in *Not Under Forty* and *Willa Cather on Writing;* also *The World of Willa Cather* by Mildred R. Bennett, *Willa Cather Living: A Personal Record* by Edith Lewis, and *Willa Cather, a Memoir* by Elizabeth Shepley Sergeant. My thanks to Alfred A. Knopf, Inc., for permission to quote from the many books by Cather first published under the Knopf imprint, as well as from Edith Lewis's recollections.

Acknowledgments

Of the poems previously unpublished in book form, a few first appeared in magazines, sometimes in slightly different versions. My thanks to the editors of *Field, The Iowa Review, Pequod,* and *The Transatlantic Review.*

I am grateful for fellowships from the John Simon Guggenheim Memorial Foundation, the Ingram Merrill Foundation, the Creative Artists Public Service Program of New York State, the National Endowment for the Arts, and the Bunting Institute of Radcliffe College, and for residencies at Blue Mountain Center and the Wurlitzer Foundation, and especially Yaddo and the MacDowell Colony, which over the years have offered privacy and community, time and the space in which to imagine and write.

Many friends have contributed to these pages—too many to name them all here. But I would like to thank in particular Barbara K. Bristol and Rodney Phillips, who scanned many drafts of previously unpublished poems; L. R. Berger, Martha Collins, Daniel Cooper, Katie Cooper, Beatrix Gates, Marie Howe, Jan Heller Levi, Susan Pliner, May Stevens, and Sally Appleton Weber for their energetic support and endlessly patient readings; and the three writers to whom this book is dedicated—Grace Paley, Adrienne Rich, and Jean Valentine—who since the late sixties have changed my life and art.

Maps & Windows was dedicated to my sister Rachel Baker, *Scaffolding* to the memory of our parents, *Green Notebook, Winter Road* to Sally Appleton Weber and in honor of Muriel Rukeyser and Shirley Eliason Haupt. The following individual poems have dedications: "The Builder of Houses" is for Sally Appleton Weber, "For a Very Old Man, on the Death of His Wife" for Sara Chermayeff, "The Earthquake" for Kay and Byron Burford, "All These Dreams" for Jean Valentine, "The Green Notebook" and "Class" for May Stevens, "My friend" for Sylvia Winner, "The Hobby Lobby" for Cynthia Macdonald, "The Past" for Martha Collins, "Wanda's Blues" for Joan Cooper, and "The Winter Road" and "Desire" for Katie Cooper.

Index